PRIMARY MATHEMATICS

TEXTBOOK 3A

Common Core Edition

SINGAPORE MATH® PROGRAM

Marshall Cavendish Education

W9-CKB-754

BLANK

Original edition published under the title Primary Mathematics Textbook 3A
© 1981 Curriculum Planning & Development Division, Ministry of Education, Singapore
Published by Times Media Private Limited

This edition © 2014 Marshall Cavendish Education Pte Ltd

Published by Marshall Cavendish Education
Times Centre, 1 New Industrial Road, Singapore 536196
Customer Service Hotline: (65) 6213 9688
US Office Tel: (1-914) 332 8888 | Fax: (1-914) 332 8882
E-mail: cs@mceducation.com
Website: www.mceducation.com

First published 2014
Reprinted 2014, 2015, 2018, 2019 (twice), 2020

Primary Mathematics (Common Core Edition) Textbook 3A
ISBN 978-981-01-9833-6

Printed in Singapore

Primary Mathematics (Common Core Edition) is adapted from Primary Mathematics Textbook 3A (3rd Edition), originally
developed by the Ministry of Education, Singapore. This edition contains new content developed by Marshall Cavendish
Education Pte Ltd, which is not attributable to the Ministry of Education, Singapore.

We would like to acknowledge the contributions by:

The Project Team from the Ministry of Education, Singapore, that developed the original Singapore Edition
Project Director: Dr Kho Tek Hong
Team Members: Hector Chee Kum Hoong, Liang Hin Hoon, Lim Eng Tann, Ng Siew Lee, Rosalind Lim Hui Cheng, Ng Hwee Wan

Primary Mathematics (Common Core Edition)
Richard Askey, Emeritus Professor of Mathematics from University of Wisconsin, Madison
Jennifer Kempe, Curriculum Advisor from Singapore Math Inc.®

PREFACE

PRIMARY MATHEMATICS Common Core Edition is a complete program from Marshall Cavendish Education, the publisher of Singapore's successful *Primary Mathematics* series. Newly adapted to align with the Common Core State Standards for mathematics, the program aims to equip students with sound concept development, critical thinking, and efficient problem-solving skills.

Mathematical concepts are introduced in the opening pages and taught to mastery through specific learning tasks that allow for immediate assessment and consolidation.

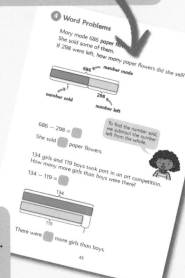

The **modeling method** enables students to visualize and solve mathematical problems quickly and efficiently.

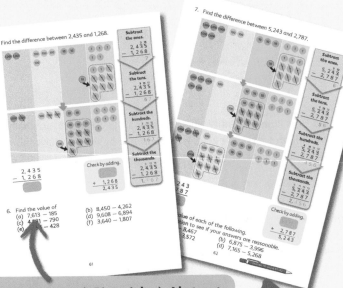

The Concrete → Pictorial → Abstract approach enables students to encounter math in a meaningful way and translate mathematical skills from the concrete to the abstract.

The **pencil icon** ✏️ Exercise 18, pages xx–xx ▷ provides quick and easy reference from the Textbook to the relevant Workbook pages. The **direct correlation** of the Workbook to the Textbook facilitates focused review and evaluation.

New mathematical concepts are introduced through a **spiral progression** that builds on concepts already taught and mastered.

③ Multiplying Ones, Tens, and Hundreds

Multiply 4 ones by 3:
4 ones × 3 = 12 ones

$4 × 3 = 12$

Multiply 4 tens by 3:
4 tens × 3 = 12 tens

$40 × 3 =$

Multiply 4 hundreds by 3:
4 hundreds × 3 = 12 hundreds

$400 × 3 =$

$4 × 3 = 12$	$40 × 3 = 120$	$400 × 3 = 1,200$
4 × 3 12	40 × 3 120	400 × 3 1,200
12 ones	12 tens	12 hundreds

96

5. Divide.
$73 ÷ 2 =$

Divide the tens by 2.

Divide the ones by 2.

When 73 is divided by 2, the quotient is ___ and the remainder is ___.

6. Numbers in which the ones digit is **0, 2, 4, 6,** or **8** are called **even numbers**.
Numbers in which the ones digit is **1, 3, 5, 7,** or **9** are called **odd numbers**.

What can you say about the remainder in each of the following?
(a) An even number divided by ___
(b) An odd number divided by ___

108

Metacognition is employed as a strategy for learners to monitor their thinking processes in problem solving. Speech and thought bubbles provide guidance through the thought processes, making even the most challenging problems accessible to students.

The color patch ▨ is used to invite active student participation and to facilitate lively discussion about the mathematical concepts taught.

REVIEW 4

1. How many legs do 9 spiders have if each spider has 8 legs?
(A) 63 (B) 72 (C) 81 (D) 90

2. What is the product of 8 hundreds and 7?
(A) 56 (B) 560 (C) 807 (D) 5,600

3. Divide 733 by 9. What is the quotient?
(A) 4 (B) 81 (C) 724 (D) 810

4. I am a number that can be divided by 3, 8 and 7. What number am I?
(A) 56 (B) 84 (C) 112 (D) 168

5. $n × 8 = ★$
$★ × 6 = 432$
What does n stand for?
(A) 9 (B) 48 (C) 72 (D) 324

6. Select True or False.
(a) $40 ÷ 8 > 20 ÷ 4$ True / False
(b) $7 × 7 = 4 ÷ 9$ True / False
(c) $0 × 9 < 2 + 0$ True / False

7. Select True or False.
(a) $32 ÷ 8 = 2 × 2$ True / False
(b) $45 − 9 > 6 × 6$ True / False
(c) $4 + 4 = 56 ÷ 7$ True / False

145

Regular **reviews** in the Textbook provide consolidation of concepts learned.

GLOSSARY

Word	Meaning
centimeter	The **centimeter** is a metric unit of length used for measuring short lengths. We write **cm** for centimeter. 100 cm = 1 m
difference	To find the **difference** between two numbers, we subtract the smaller number from the greater number. $142 − 21 = 121$ The **difference** between 142 and 21 is 121.
estimation	When we **estimate** an answer, we round the parts of the question so that we can find an answer quickly. This gives us an answer that is about the same as the actual answer. 312 + 48 is about 300 + 50. Thus, the value of 312 + 48 is about $300 + 50 = 350$

173

The **Glossary** effectively combines pictorial representation with simple mathematical definitions to provide a comprehensive reference guide for students.

CONTENTS

1 NUMBERS TO 10,000

1 Thousands, Hundreds, Tens, and Ones

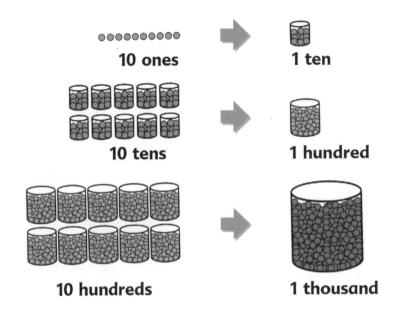

10 ones → 1 ten

10 tens → 1 hundred

10 hundreds → 1 thousand

(a) Sam collected some marbles.

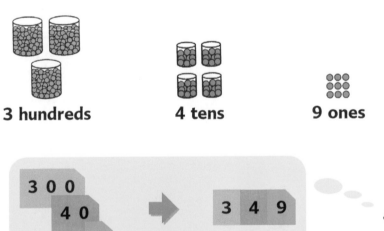

3 hundreds   4 tens   9 ones

3 0 0
  4 0
    9 → 3 4 9

300 + 40 + 9 = ☐

(b) His sister also collected some marbles.

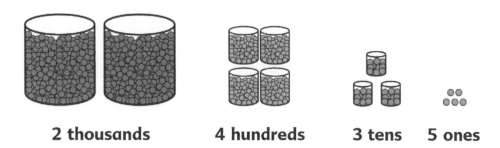

2 thousands   **4 hundreds**   **3 tens**   **5 ones**

2,000 + 400 + 30 + 5 =

How many marbles did she collect?

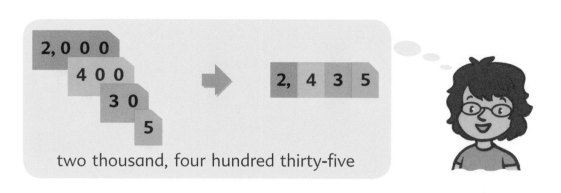

2,0 0 0
4 0 0
3 0
5

➡ 2, 4 3 5

two thousand, four hundred thirty-five

2,000 + 400 + 30 + 5 is the **expanded form** of 2,435.

2,435 is the **standard form**.

(c) Read the numbers 5,998 and 6,012.

(d) Count from 5,998 to 6,012.

5,998, 5,999, 6,000, ..., 6,012

(e) Count from 9,987 to 10,000.

1. Count the thousands, hundreds, tens, and ones in this chart.

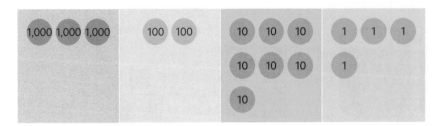

$3,000 + 200 + 70 + 4 =$

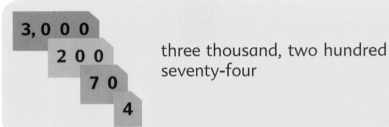

three thousand, two hundred seventy-four

2. What numbers are shown below?
Read each number.
Write each number in standard form, expanded form, and in words.

(a)

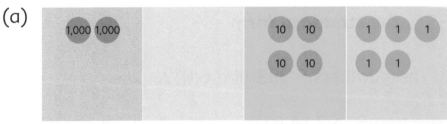

(b)

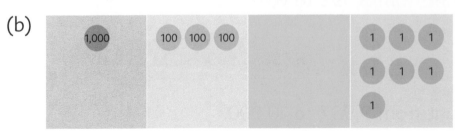

(c)

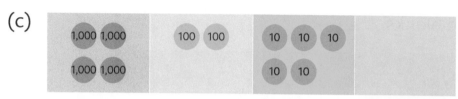

(d)

3. Write the numbers in standard form.
   (a) two thousand, one hundred sixty-three
   (b) eight thousand, eight
   (c) five thousand, three hundred
   (d) six thousand, forty

Exercise 1, pages 6–8

4.
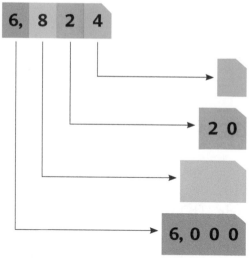

6,824 is a 4-digit number.
The digit 2 stands for 20.
The digit 6 stands for 6,000.
What does the digit 8 stand for?
What does the digit 4 stand for?

5. What does the digit **5** stand for in each of the following numbers?
   (a) 3,**5**21   (b) **5**,213   (c) 1,2**5**3

6. Fill in the blanks.

Thousands	Hundreds	Tens	Ones
3	4	6	8

In 3,468, the digit 8 is in the **ones place**. Its **value** is 8.

The digit 6 is in the **tens place**. Its value is 60.

The digit is in the **hundreds place**. Its value is .

The digit ⬜ is in the **thousands place**. Its value is ⬜.

7. What is the value of each digit in 8,137?

8. (a) How many hundreds are in 6,241?

6,241 = 6,200 + 41

There are 62 hundreds in 6,241.

(b) How many tens are there in 6,241?

6,241 = 6,240 + 1

There are ⬜ tens in 6,241.

9. Fill in the blanks.

(a) 8,401 has ⬜ thousands. (b) 1,903 has ⬜ hundreds.

(c) 6,514 has ⬜ tens. (d) 4,056 has ⬜ ones.

10. What is each number in standard form?

(a) 3 thousands + 15 tens = ⬜

(b) 42 hundreds + 78 ones = ⬜

(c) 20 hundreds + 60 tens + 93 ones = ⬜

Exercise 2, pages 9–10

12

11. Which is greater, 316 or 264?

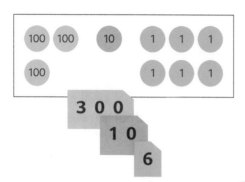

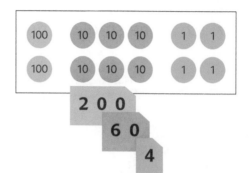

316 is greater than 264.

Compare the hundreds.
300 is greater than 200.
So, 316 > 264.

Which is smaller, 325 or 352?

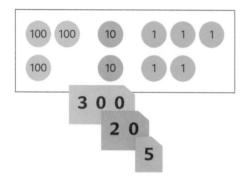

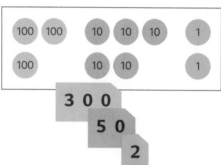

325 is smaller than 352.

When the hundreds are the same, compare the tens.
20 < 50
So, 325 < 352.

(a) Which is greater, 4,316 or 4,264?
    Which is greater, 4,316 or 5,264?
(b) Which is smaller, 2,325 or 2,352?
    Which is smaller, 3,325 or 2,352?

12. Which sign goes in each ⬤ , >, <, or =?

(a) 7,031 ⬤ 7,301   (b) 8,004 ⬤ 8,040

(c) 3,756 ⬤ 3,576   (d) 5,698 ⬤ 5,698

13. 5,073   4,982   4,973

Which is the greatest number?
Which is the smallest number?

14.

100 is the smallest
3-digit number.

999 is the greatest
3-digit number.

What is the smallest 4-digit number?
What is the greatest 4-digit number?

15. Arrange the numbers in order.
Begin with the greatest.

3,412   3,142   4,123   2,431

16. Arrange the numbers in order.
Begin with the smallest.

1,892   9,003   913   1,703

17. Use all the digits 0, 4, and 5 to
make different 3-digit numbers.
Which is the greatest number?
Which is the smallest number?

Do not begin a
number with 0.

18. (a) What is the greatest 4-digit number that you can make
using all the digits 0, 7, 2, and 8?

(b) What is the smallest 4-digit number that you can make
using all the digits 3, 7, 4, and 9?

Exercise 3, pages 11—12

2 Number Patterns

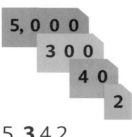

5, **3** 4 2

5, **4** 4 2

Which is more? How many more?

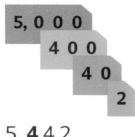

5, **4** 4 2

5, **5** 4 2

Which is more? How many more?

What number is 100 more than 5,442?

What number is 100 more than 5,542?

Complete the following regular number patterns.

(a) 5,**3**42, 5,**4**42, 5,**5**42,   ,

(b) **5**,342, **6**,342, **7**,342,   ,

(c) 5,34**2**, 5,34**3**, 5,34**4**,   ,

(d) 5,3**4**2, 5,3**5**2, 5,3**6**2,

$$5,342 \xrightarrow{\ +100\ } 5,442$$

$$5,442 \xrightarrow{\ +100\ } 5,542$$

$$5,542 \xrightarrow{\ +?\ } ?$$

1. (a) What number is 100 more than 3,624?

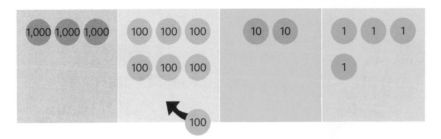

3,624 $\xrightarrow{+100}$ ▢

Add 1 hundred to 3,624.

(b) What number is 1 more than 3,624?

(c) What number is 10 more than 3,624?

(d) What number is 1,000 more than 3,624?

2. (a) What number is 1,000 less than 5,732?

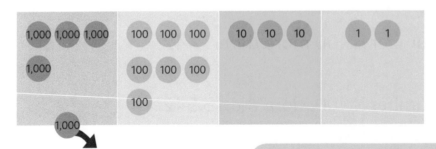

5,732 $\xrightarrow{-1,000}$ ▢

Subtract 1 thousand from 5,732.

(b) What number is 1 less than 5,732?

(c) What number is 10 less than 5,732?

(d) What number is 100 less than 5,732?

3. (a) Count by 10s from 1,678 to 1,728.
   1,678,   1,688,   1,698,   ...,   1,728

   (b) Count by 100s from 1,678 to 2,178.
   1,678,   1,778,   1,878,   ...,   2,178

   (c) Count by 1,000s from 1,678 to 8,678.
   1,678,   2,678,   3,678,   ...,   8,678

4. Complete the following regular number patterns.

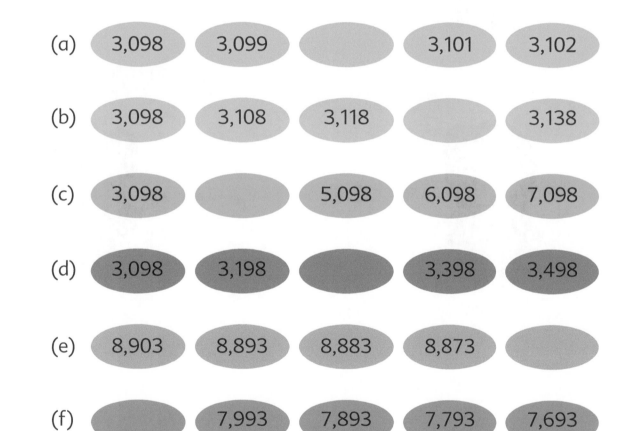

(a) 3,098   3,099   3,101   3,102

(b) 3,098   3,108   3,118   3,138

(c) 3,098   5,098   6,098   7,098

(d) 3,098   3,198   3,398   3,498

(e) 8,903   8,893   8,883   8,873

(f)   7,993   7,893   7,793   7,693

Exercise 4, pages 13—15

③ Rounding Numbers

I save about $60.

Maggie

Our Savings

Maggie	$61
Rosa	$68
Brandy	$75

I save about $80.

Brandy

I save about $70.

Rosa

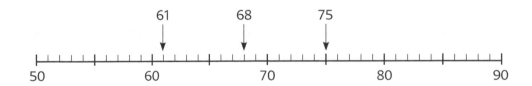

They **round** each of the numbers 61, 68, and 75 to the nearest ten.

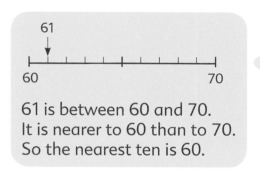

61 is between 60 and 70.
It is nearer to 60 than to 70.
So the nearest ten is 60.

61 is 60 when rounded to the nearest ten.

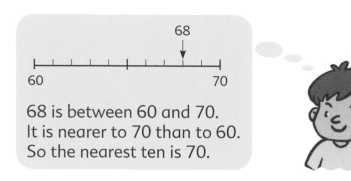

68 is between 60 and 70.
It is nearer to 70 than to 60.
So the nearest ten is 70.

68 is 70 when rounded to the nearest ten.

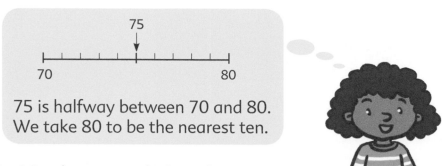

75 is halfway between 70 and 80.
We take 80 to be the nearest ten.

75 is 80 when rounded to the nearest ten.

1. Round each number to the nearest ten.
   (a) 29   (b) 38   (c) 82   (d) 95

2. Round each number to the nearest ten.
   (a) 234

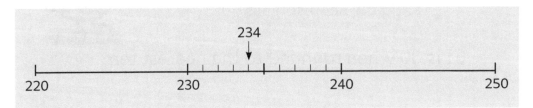

   234 is between 230 and 240.
   234 is nearer to 230 than to 240.

   234 is [ ] when rounded to the nearest ten.

   (b) 1,458

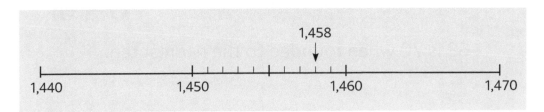

   1,458 is between 1,450 and 1,460.
   1,458 is nearer to 1,460 than to 1,450.
   1,458 is [ ] when rounded to the nearest ten.

   (c) 2,735

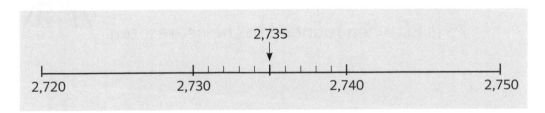

   2,735 is halfway between 2,730 and 2,740.

   2,735 is [ ] when rounded to the nearest ten.

3. Round each number to the nearest ten.
   (a) 129   (b) 201   (c) 452   (d) 685
   (e) 2,069   (f) 4,355   (g) 4,805   (h) 5,508

Exercise 5, pages 16—17

4. There are 2,478 students in Lakeview School.
   (a) Round the number of students to the nearest ten.

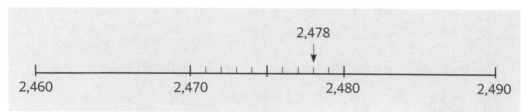

2,478 is more than halfway between 2,470 and 2,480.
It is nearer to 2,480 than to 2,470.

2,478 is [ ] when rounded to the nearest ten.

   (b) Round the number of students to the nearest hundred.

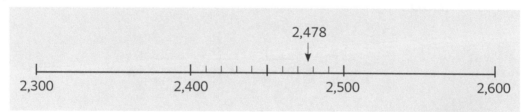

2,478 is more than halfway between 2,400 and 2,500.
It is nearer to 2,500 than to 2,400.

2,478 is when rounded to the nearest hundred.

21

5. Mr. Ricci sold his car for $9,125.
   Round this amount to the nearest $100.

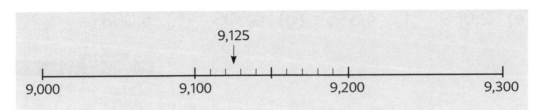

$9,125 is $ ▢ when rounded to the nearest $100.

6. Round each number to the nearest hundred.

   (a) 345

   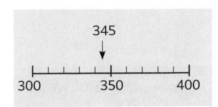

   (b) 3,670

   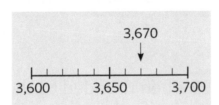

   (c) 4,850

   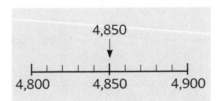

7. Round each number to the nearest hundred.
   (a) 320   (b) 486   (c) 650   (d) 980

   (e) 2,915   (f) 3,075   (g) 4,308   (h) 5,150

   (i) 9,234   (j) 8,520   (k) 7,450   (l) 9,990

Exercise 6, pages 18–19

8. There were 7,355 people at a football game.

   (a) Round 7,355 to the nearest ten.

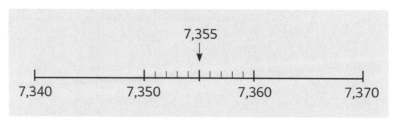

   7,355 is halfway between 7,350 and 7,360.

   7,355 is ⬜ when rounded to the nearest ten.

   (b) Round 7,355 to the nearest hundred.

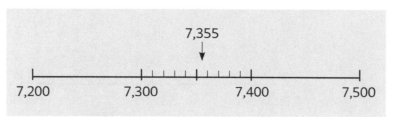

   7,355 is ⬜ when rounded to the nearest hundred.

   (c) Round 7,355 to the nearest thousand.

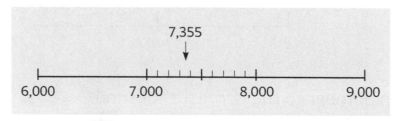

   7,355 is ⬜ when rounded to the nearest thousand.

9. Round each number to the nearest thousand.

   (a) 4,800

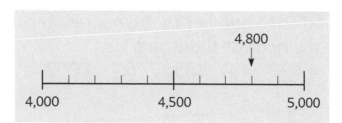

(b) 7,455

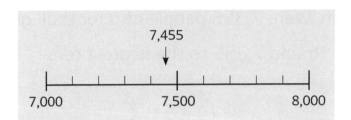

(c) 3,010

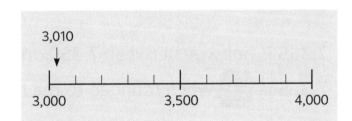

(d) 8,500

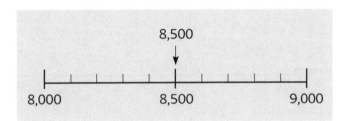

(e) 9,580

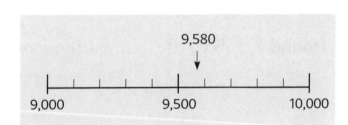

10. Round each number to the nearest thousand.
   (a) 2,680   (b) 8,980   (c) 6,499   (d) 3,508
   (e) 3,058   (f) 1,280   (g) 1,800   (h) 5,075
   (i) 8,765   (j) 9,705   (k) 9,052   (l) 7,501

11. Round each number to the nearest ten, the nearest hundred, and the nearest thousand.
   (a) 4,497   (b) 385   (c) 4,002

Exercise 7, pages 20–21

REVIEW 1

1. Which of the following is equal to 679?
   (A) 600 + 700 + 900
   (B) 6 + 70 + 900
   (C) 600 + 70 + 9
   (D) 6 + 7 + 9

2. Nine thousand, nine hundred and nine is the same as _____.
   (A) 9,099
   (B) 9,909
   (C) 9,990
   (D) 9,999

3. What is the value of the digit 3 in 1,038?
   (A) 3
   (B) 30
   (C) 300
   (D) 3000

4. How many tens are there in 4,526?
   (A) 2
   (B) 20
   (C) 52
   (D) 452

5. What is 74 hundreds and 2 tens in standard form?
   (A) 76
   (B) 742
   (C) 7,402
   (D) 7,420

6. Select True or False.
   (a) 871 < 800 + 70 + 2   True / False
   (b) 1,000 + 600 + 3 = 1,063   True / False

7. Select True or False.
   (a) 10 less than 7,234 is 7,244.   True / False
   (b) 100 more than 4,906 is 5,006.   True / False

8. What number is shown in each of the following?

   (a) 1,000 100 100 1 1 1 1 1

   (b) 1,000 1,000 1,000 10 10

   (c) 1,000 1,000 10 10 10 1 1

9. Write the numbers in words.
   (a) 1,347   (b) 6,052

10. Write the numbers in expanded form.
    (a) 1,736   (b) 7,504

11. Write the underlined words in standard form.
    (a) The height of Mount Columbia in Colorado is <u>four thousand, two hundred ninety-one</u> meters.
    (b) Mr. Ward bought a computer for <u>two thousand, sixty</u> dollars.

12. What does each digit in 8,072 stand for?

13. Fill in the blanks.

    (a) In 5,619, the digit 6 is in the ⬜ place. Its value is ⬜.

    (b) In 8,305, the digit 0 is in the ⬜ place. Its value is ⬜.

    (c) In 4,527, the digit 4 is in the ⬜ place. Its value is ⬜.

14. (a) How many thousands are there in 5,406?
    (b) How many hundreds are there in 5,406?
    (c) How many tens are there in 5,406?
    (d) How many ones are there in 5,406?

15. Which sign goes in the ⬤ , > or <?

    (a) 7,865 ⬤ 8,567

    (b) 4,104 ⬤ 4,049

16. Which is the greatest number?
    7,171   7,711   7,117

17. Arrange these numbers in order.
    Begin with the smallest.

18. Arrange these numbers in order.
    Begin with the smallest.

19. What is the greatest 4-digit number that you can make using all the digits 5, 0, 9, and 1?

20. What is the smallest 4-digit number that you can make using all the digits 8, 4, 7, and 2?

21. Which sign goes in the ⬤ , >, <, or =?

    (a) 5,520 ⬤ 5,420

    (b) 3,510 ⬤ 3,590

    (c) 4,907 ⬤ 4,907

    (d) 6,990 ⬤ 6,790

22. Write the next two numbers for the following number pattern.

    2,007,   2,008,   2,009,   ⬜ ,   ⬜

23. Complete the following regular number patterns.

    (a) 996, 997, 998, 999, ⬜

    (b) 4,115, 4,015, 3,915, ⬜ , 3,715

    (c) 2,080, ⬜ , 2,100, 2,110, 2,120

    (d) 5,103, 6,103, ⬜ , 8,103, 9,103

    (e) ⬜ , 5,978, 5,878, 5,778, 5,678

24. Round each number to the nearest ten.
    (a) 93
    (b) 302
    (c) 915
    (d) 3,487

25. Round each number to the nearest hundred.
    (a) 560
    (b) 650
    (c) 8,902
    (d) 2,392

26. Round each number to the nearest thousand.
    (a) 4,502
    (b) 5,934
    (c) 3,042
    (d) 6,755

27. Round 6,497 to the nearest
    (a) ten,
    (b) hundred,
    (c) thousand.

28. Which is greater, 985 or 1,042?
    Steve drew the following and explained that 985 is greater
    because we should always compare the first digit.

    9 8 5

    1 0 4 2

    9 is greater than 1. So, 985 must be greater than 1,042.
    Is he correct? Explain your answer.

Review 1, pages 22–27

2 ADDITION AND SUBTRACTION

1 Mental Calculation

What number is 3 more than 42?

42 + 3

10 1   1

10 1   1

10   1

10

42 + 3 = ☐

2 + 3 < 10

I can add the ones.
42 + 3
 / \
40   2

2 + 3 = 5
40 + 5 = 45

What number is 5 more than 38?
Add 38 and 5.

10 1 1   1

10 1 1   1

10 1 1   1

    1   1

    1   1

38 + 5 = ☐
        / \
       2   3

8 and 5 will be
greater than 10.

Make a 10 first.
38 + 5
 / \
2   3

38 + 2 = 40
40 + 3 = 43

1. Add.
   (a) 59 + 8
   (b) 41 + 9
   (c) 34 + 5
   (d) 82 + 7
   (e) 39 + 4
   (f) 17 + 7

2. Add 46 and 27.

46   **27**

46 + 27

$$46 + 27$$
$$\diagup \quad \diagdown$$
20   7

Add 20 to 46 first.

46 $\xrightarrow{+20}$ 66 $\xrightarrow{+7}$ 73

46 + 27 = ▢

3. Add 58 and 16.

58 + 16 = ▢

58 + 16

$$58 + 16$$
$$\diagup \quad \diagdown$$
2   14

58 + 2 = 60

60 + 14 = ▢

4. Add.
   (a) 23 + 14
   (b) 54 + 36
   (c) 38 + 45

5. Add 26 and 49.

26 + 49 =

49 is 1 less than 50.

So, adding 49 is the same as adding 50 and subtracting 1.

$$26 \xrightarrow{+50} 76 \xrightarrow{-1} 75$$

6. Add.
   (a) 39 + 8   (b) 58 + 34   (c) 45 + 65
   (d) 78 + 14   (e) 39 + 27   (f) 53 + 18

Exercise 1, pages 28–29

7. (a) What number is 3 more than 8?
   (b) What number is 30 more than 80?
   (c) What number is 30 more than 84?
   (d) What number is 3 more than 28?
   (e) What number is 30 more than 280?
   (f) What number is 30 more than 284?

8. Add.
   (a) 43 + 30   (b) 67 + 40   (c) 82 + 30
   (d) 78 + 40   (e) 78 + 41   (f) 78 + 42
   (g) 240 + 60   (h) 240 + 70   (i) 240 + 72

9. Add 483 and 98.

483 + 98 =

98 is 2 less than 100.

So, adding 98 is the same as adding 100 and subtracting 2.

$$483 \xrightarrow{+100} 583 \xrightarrow{-2} 581$$

10. Add.
    (a) 48 + 99   (b) 348 + 98   (c) 560 + 99
    (d) 78 + 97   (e) 458 + 97   (f) 560 + 95

Exercise 2, page 30

11. Subtract 4 from 30.

$30 - 4$

20   10

$10 - 4 = 6$
$20 + 6 = 26$

So, $30 - 4 = 26$.

$30 - 4 = $

12. Subtract 8 from 41.

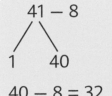

$41 - 8$

1   40

$40 - 8 = 32$
$32 + 1 = 33$
So, $41 - 8 = 33$.

I do it this way:

$41 - 1 = 40$
$40 - 7 = 33$
So, $41 - 8 = 33$.

$41 - 8 = $

13. Subtract.
   (a) $60 - 5$ (b) $32 - 6$ (c) $87 - 9$
   (d) $48 - 5$ (e) $62 - 7$ (f) $45 - 3$

14. Subtract 34 from 87.

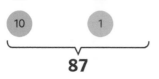

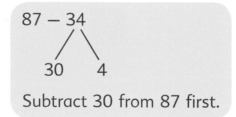

87 $\xrightarrow{-30}$ 57 $\xrightarrow{-4}$ 53

87 − 34 = ☐

15. Subtract.
    (a) 65 − 12   (b) 76 − 46   (c) 63 − 28

16. Subtract 18 from 90.

90 − 18 = ☐

90 − 18

70   20

20 − 18 = 2
90 − 18 = 70 + 2

Another way:
90 − 18 = 90 − 20 + 2

17. Subtract.
    (a) 30 − 28   (b) 60 − 56   (c) 70 − 65
    (d) 50 − 17   (e) 40 − 29   (f) 80 − 58
    (g) 40 − 16   (h) 70 − 47   (i) 90 − 39

Exercise 3, pages 31–32

18. Subtract 49 from 86.

$86 - 49 = \boxed{}$

49 is 1 less than 50.

So, subtracting 49 is the same as subtracting 50 and adding 1.

$86 \xrightarrow{-50} 36 \xrightarrow{+1} 37$

19. Subtract.
    (a) $73 - 49$ (b) $85 - 38$ (c) $35 - 19$
    (d) $156 - 38$ (e) $249 - 58$ (f) $94 - 27$

20. (a) What number is 7 less than 13?
    (b) What number is 70 less than 130?
    (c) What number is 7 less than 43?
    (d) What number is 70 less than 430?
    (e) What number is 70 less than 435?

21. Subtract.
    (a) $14 - 8$ (b) $140 - 80$ (c) $142 - 80$
    (d) $430 - 30$ (e) $430 - 80$ (f) $435 - 80$
    (g) $800 - 70$ (h) $820 - 70$ (i) $821 - 70$
    (j) $120 - 50$ (k) $432 - 60$ (l) $689 - 50$

22. Subtract 98 from 483.

$483 - 98 = \boxed{}$

98 is 2 less than 100.

So, subtracting 98 is the same as subtracting 100 and adding 2.

$483 \xrightarrow{-100} 383 \xrightarrow{+2} 385$

23. Subtract.
    (a) $546 - 98$ (b) $235 - 99$ (c) $992 - 97$
    (d) $286 - 98$ (e) $349 - 96$ (f) $872 - 95$

Exercise 4, page 33

24. 9 tens and 10 ones make 100.

30 + 60 = 90
      = 9 tens

7 + 3 = 10
     = 1 ten

37 + 63 = 100

25. What number goes in the ⬜ ?

(a) 29 + ⬜ = 100

(b) 129 + ⬜ = 200

(c) 94 + ⬜ = 100

(d) 394 + ⬜ = 400

(e) 100 − 88 = ⬜

(f) 200 − 188 = ⬜

(g) 100 − 47 = ⬜

(h) 300 − 247 = ⬜

26. 9 hundreds, 9 tens, and 10 ones make 1,000.

600 + 300 = 900
       = 9 hundreds

80 + 10 = 90
     = 9 tens

5 + 5 = 10
     = 1 ten

685 + 315 = 1,000

27. What number goes in the ⬜ ?

(a) 265 + ⬜ = 1,000

(b) 1,265 + ⬜ = 2,000

(c) 83 + ⬜ = 1,000

(d) 5,083 + ⬜ = 6,000

(e) 7 + ⬜ = 1,000

(f) 2,007 + ⬜ = 3,000

(g) 1,000 − 482 = ⬜

(h) 1,000 − 507 = ⬜

Exercise 5, pages 34–35

② Looking Back: Addition and Subtraction

(a) Add 625 and 218. Estimate the answer first.

```
  2 1 8
+ 6 2 5
───────
```

218 is about 200.
625 is about 600.

200 + 600 = 800

The answer should be about 800.

Add the ones.

```
   1
  2 1 8
+ 6 2 5
───────
      3
```

Add the tens.

```
   1
  2 1 8
+ 6 2 5
───────
    4 3
```

Add the hundreds.

```
   1
  2 1 8
+ 6 2 5
───────
  8 4 3
```

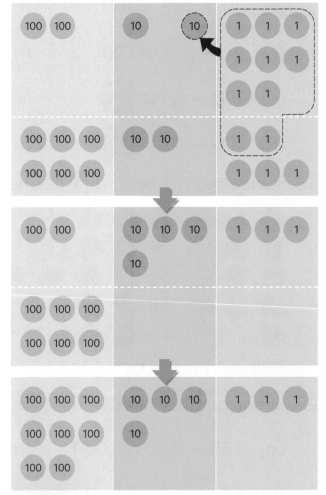

Is the answer reasonable?

843 is close to the estimated answer of 800.

The answer is reasonable.

(b) Subtract 267 from 453. Estimate the answer first.

$$
\begin{array}{r}
4\,5\,3 \\
-\ 2\,6\,7 \\
\hline
\end{array}
$$

453 is about 500.
267 is about 300.

$500 - 300 = 200$

The answer is reasonable if it is about 200.

Subtract the ones.

$$
\begin{array}{r}
4\ \overset{4}{\cancel{5}}\ \overset{13}{\cancel{3}} \\
-\ 2\ 6\ 7 \\
\hline
6
\end{array}
$$

Subtract the tens.

$$
\begin{array}{r}
\overset{3}{\cancel{4}}\ \overset{14}{\cancel{5}}\ \overset{13}{\cancel{3}} \\
-\ 2\ 6\ 7 \\
\hline
8\ 6
\end{array}
$$

Subtract the hundreds.

$$
\begin{array}{r}
\overset{3}{\cancel{4}}\ \overset{14}{\cancel{5}}\ \overset{13}{\cancel{3}} \\
-\ 2\ 6\ 7 \\
\hline
1\ 8\ 6
\end{array}
$$

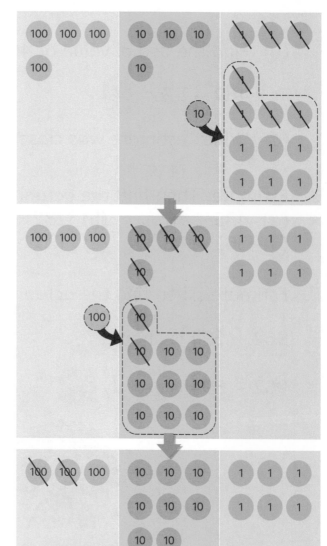

Is the answer reasonable?

We can also check our answer with addition.

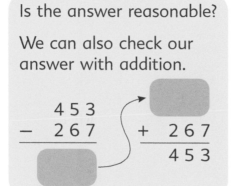

1. (a) Estimate the value of 469 – 52.

469 is about 500.
52 is about 50.

500 – 50 = 450

469 is about 470.
52 is about 50.

470 – 50 = 420

```
    4 6 9
 –    5 2
 _____
```

(b) Find the actual value of 469 – 52.

469 – 52 =

(c) Which estimate was closer, 450 or 420?

2. Estimate. Then find the actual value of
   (a) 435 + 48   (b) 282 + 27   (c) 925 + 67
   (d) 362 – 48   (e) 123 – 58   (f) 304 – 76

3. Estimate. Then find the actual value of 962 – 594.

962 – 594 is about ▢.

962 – 594 is exactly ▢.

I can check my answer by adding.

```
    9 6 2            + 5 9 4
 –  5 9 4            _____
 _____             9 6 2
```

4. Find the value of each of the following.
   Use estimation to see if your answers are reasonable.
   (a) 726 + 258   (b) 374 + 481   (c) 484 + 166
   (d) 906 – 524   (e) 695 – 167   (f) 813 – 325

Exercise 6, pages 36–37

3 Sum and Difference

134 girls and 119 boys took part in an art competition.

(a) How many children took part in the competition?

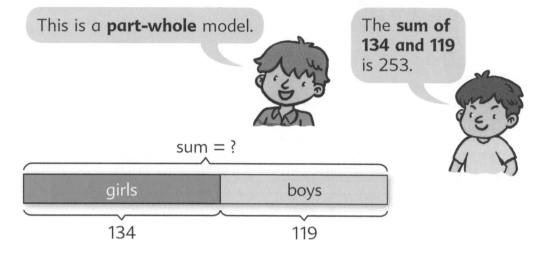

This is a **part-whole** model.

The **sum of 134 and 119** is 253.

sum = ?

| girls | boys |
| 134 | 119 |

134 + 119 = 253

[ ] children took part in the art competition.

(b) How many more girls than boys were there?

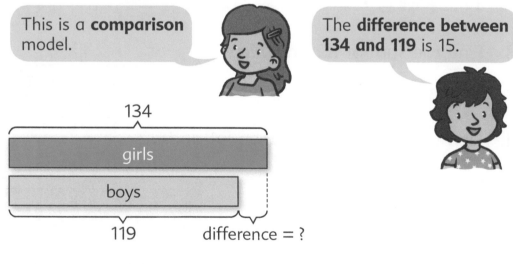

This is a **comparison** model.

The **difference between 134 and 119** is 15.

134

girls

boys

119   difference = ?

134 − 119 = 15

There were [ ] more girls than boys.

1. Fill in the blanks.

(a) $8 + 5 = \boxed{}$

The sum of 8 and 5 is $\boxed{}$.

(b) $8 - 5 = \boxed{}$

The difference between 8 and 5 is $\boxed{}$.

2. Complete the equations.

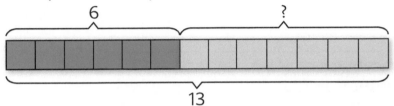

$13 - \boxed{} = 6$ $13 - 6 = \boxed{}$

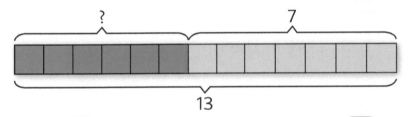

$13 - \boxed{} = 7$ $13 - 7 = \boxed{}$

3. Find the sum of 89 and 76.

$89 + 76 = \boxed{}$

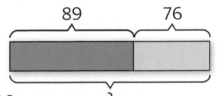

4. Find the difference between 54 and 90.

$90 - 54 = \boxed{}$

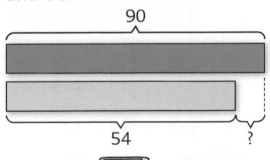

Exercise 7, pages 38–39

5. 40 + 25 = ▢

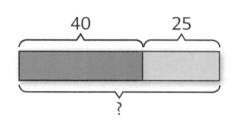

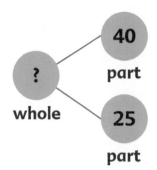

To find the whole, we add.

6. 32 + ▢ = 45

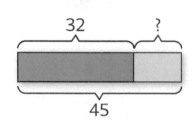

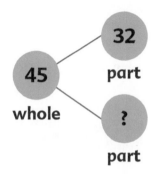

To find a part, we subtract.

45 − 32 = ▢

7. (a) 85 − ▢ = 40

To find a part, we subtract.

85 − 40 = ▢

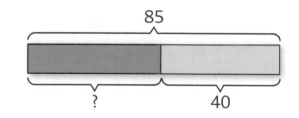

(b) ▢ − 24 = 68

To find the whole, we add.

68 + 24 = ▢

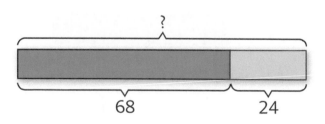

8. What number goes in the  ?

(a) $76 + \boxed{} = 84$

(b) $72 - \boxed{} = 66$

(c) $84 - \boxed{} = 69$

(d) $\boxed{} + 34 = 87$

(e) $\boxed{} - 22 = 60$

(f) $\boxed{} - 41 = 27$

(g) $80 - \boxed{} = 30 + 20$

(h) $15 + \boxed{} = 20 - 1$

(i) $\boxed{} + 406 = 592$

(j) $592 - \boxed{} = 421$

(k) $\boxed{} - 123 = 402$

Exercise 8, pages 40–41

9. (a) How much more than 23 is 85?

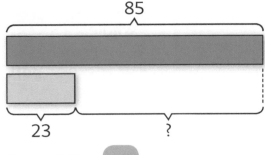

We need to find the difference between 85 and 23.

$85 = 23 + \boxed{}$

$85 - 23 = \boxed{}$

85 is $\boxed{}$ more than 23.

(b) How much less than 90 is 62?

We can use a letter instead of $\boxed{}$ or ? for the unknown number.

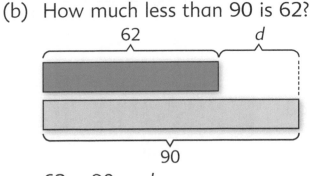

$62 = 90 - d$

$90 - 62 = d$

$d = \boxed{}$

62 is $\boxed{}$ less than 90.

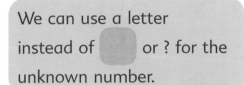

10. How much more than 241 is 513?

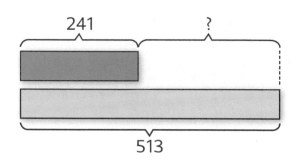

$241 + \boxed{} = 513$

$513 - 241 = \boxed{}$

513 is $\boxed{}$ more than 241.

11. (a) What is 24 more than 21? (b) 29 is 14 less than what number?

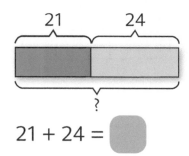

$21 + 24 = \boxed{}$

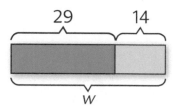

$29 = w - 14$

$29 + 14 = w$

$w = \boxed{}$

12. Solve.

(a) 9 more than 49 is $\boxed{}$.

(b) 12 more than $\boxed{}$ is 45.

(c) $\boxed{}$ more than 62 is 99.

(d) 38 is $\boxed{}$ less than 342.

(e) 20 less than $\boxed{}$ is 36.

(f) $\boxed{}$ more than 183 is 304.

(g) $\boxed{}$ less than 90 is 55.

(h) 78 more than $\boxed{}$ is 200.

Exercise 9, pages 42—43

13. Which sign goes in each , **>**, **<**, or **=**?

(a) 6 + 1 ⬤ 6 + 3

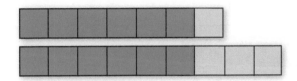

(b) 14 + 5 ⬤ 14 + 8

(c) 23 + 81 ⬤ 38 + 81

14. Which sign goes in each ⬤, **>**, **<**, or **=**?

(a) 10 − 5 ⬤ 10 − 6

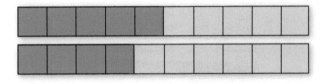

(b) 12 − 7 ⬤ 12 − 3

(c) 86 − 15 ⬤ 86 − 17

15. Which sign goes in each ⬤, **>**, **<**, or **=**?

(a) 23 + 5 ⬤ 23 − 5   (b) 82 + 10 ⬤ 92 − 10

(c) 45 − 12 ⬤ 45 − 32   (d) 14 + 26 ⬤ 43 + 9

(e) 32 + 48 ⬤ 61 − 18   (f) 36 + 47 ⬤ 36 + 29

(g) 87 + 6 ⬤ 28 − 14   (h) 62 + 21 ⬤ 72 + 11

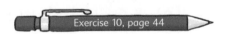

Exercise 10, page 44

4 Word Problems

Mary made 686 paper flowers.
She sold some of them.
If 298 were left, how many paper flowers did she sell?

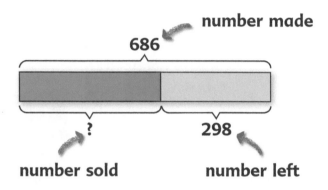

number made
686

? **298**

number sold **number left**

To find the number sold,
we subtract the number
left from the whole.

$686 - 298 =$ ▢

She sold ▢ paper flowers.

134 girls and 119 boys took part in an art competition.
How many more girls than boys were there?

$134 - 119 =$ ▢

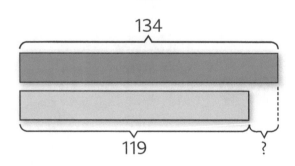

134

119 ?

There were ▢ more girls than boys.

1. A man sold 230 balloons at a carnival in the morning.
   He sold another 86 balloons in the evening.
   How many balloons did he sell in all?

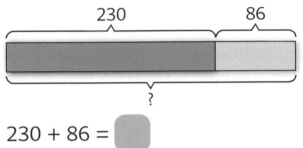

230 is about 200.
86 is about 100.

$200 + 100 = 300$

The answer is reasonable if it is near 300.

$230 + 86 = $ ☐

He sold ☐ balloons in all.

2. The sum of two numbers is 175.
   If one number is 49, what is the other number?

$49 + p = 175$

$175 - 49 = p$

$p = $ ☐

The other number is ☐.

3. Lynn saved $184.
   She saved $63 more than Betty.
   How much did Betty save?

I can check my answer with addition.

$\$184 - \$63 = \$$ ☐

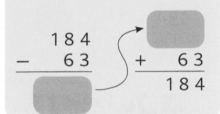

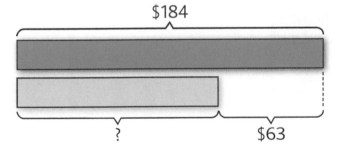

Betty saved $ ☐.

46

4. 627 boys and 493 girls took part in a storytelling competition.
How many children took part in the storytelling competition altogether?

children took part in the storytelling competition.

5. There were 945 musical tickets for sale in the morning.
808 tickets were sold at the end of the day.
How many tickets were left?

tickets were left.

6.

Xylophone A

Xylophone B

How much more does Xylophone A cost than Xylophone B?

Xylophone A costs more than Xylophone B.

7. After spending $134 on a table, Claire had $265 left.
How much did she have at first?

She had at first.

Exercise 11, pages 45—47

8. John read 32 pages in the morning.
   He read 14 fewer pages in the afternoon.
   (a) How many pages did he read in the afternoon?
   (b) How many pages did he read altogether?

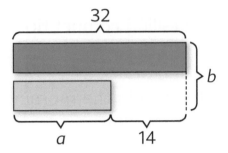

(a) $32 - 14 = a$

   $a = $ ⬜

   He read ⬜ pages in the afternoon.

(b) $32 + a = b$

   $b = $ ⬜

   He read ⬜ pages altogether.

9. The difference between two numbers is 68. The smaller
   number is 153.
   (a) What is the greater number?
   (b) What is the sum of the two numbers?

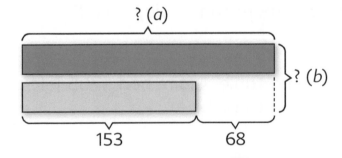

(a) The greater number is ⬜.

(b) The sum of the two numbers is ⬜.

10. 950 people were at a magic show.
    406 of them were men.
    232 were children.
    The rest were women.
    (a) How many men and children were there?
    (b) How many women were there?

11. Kyle folded 218 paper cranes for his Art project on Saturday.
    He folded 96 fewer paper cranes on Sunday than on
    Saturday.
    (a) How many paper cranes did he fold on Sunday?
    (b) How many paper cranes did he fold altogether?

12. There were 713 people at a dog show.
    402 of them were adults.
    The rest were children.
    (a) How many children were there?
    (b) How many more adults than children were there?

Exercise 12, pages 48–50

5 Adding Ones, Tens, Hundreds, and Thousands

Add.

$1,736 + 2 =$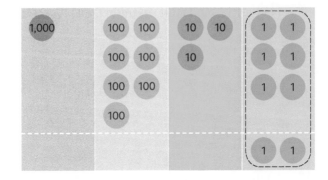

$$
\begin{array}{r}
1,7\,3\,6 \\
+ \qquad 2 \\
\hline
\end{array}
$$

$4,028 + 50 =$

$$
\begin{array}{r}
4,0\,2\,8 \\
+ \qquad 5\,0 \\
\hline
\end{array}
$$

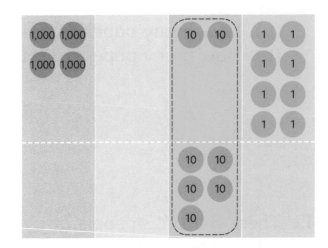

$7,245 + 600 =$

$$
\begin{array}{r}
7,2\,4\,5 \\
+ \qquad 6\,0\,0 \\
\hline
\end{array}
$$

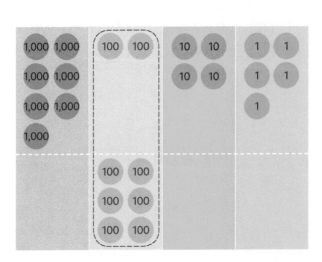

$6{,}912 + 3{,}000 =$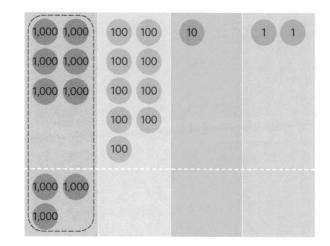

$$\begin{array}{r} 6{,}9\,1\,2 \\ +\ \ 3{,}0\,0\,0 \\ \hline \end{array}$$

$5{,}361 + 4{,}307 =$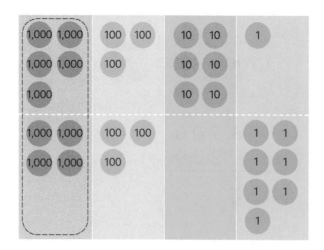

$$\begin{array}{r} 5{,}3\,6\,1 \\ +\ \ 4{,}3\,0\,7 \\ \hline \end{array}$$

$2{,}048 + 2 =$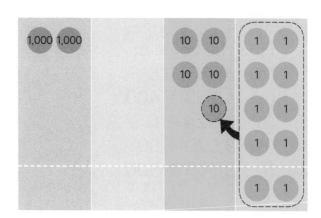

$$\begin{array}{r} 2{,}0\,4\,8 \\ +\ \ \ \ \ \ 2 \\ \hline \end{array}$$

$5,840 + 60 =$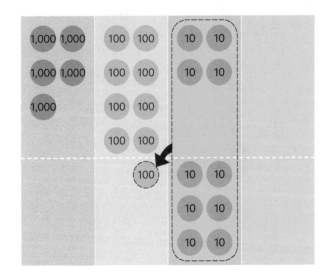

$$
\begin{array}{r}
5,840 \\
+60 \\
\hline
\end{array}
$$

$3,700 + 300 =$

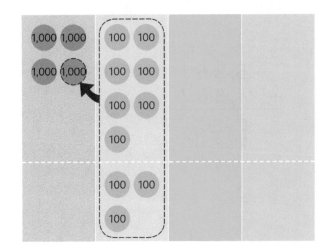

$$
\begin{array}{r}
3,700 \\
+300 \\
\hline
\end{array}
$$

1. Find the value of
   (a) 4,263 + 5
   (b) 4,263 + 20
   (c) 4,263 + 400
   (d) 4,263 + 3,000
   (e) 3,524 + 6
   (f) 3,574 + 6
   (g) 3,520 + 80
   (h) 3,524 + 80
   (i) 3,500 + 500
   (j) 3,524 + 500

Exercise 13, pages 51–52

2. Find the sum of 2,803 and 1,443.

$$\begin{array}{r} 2,803 \\ +\ 1,443 \\ \hline \end{array}$$

Estimate the answer by rounding to the nearest thousand.

$$\begin{array}{r} 2,803 \longrightarrow\ \ \ 3,000 \\ 1,443 \longrightarrow +\ \ 1,000 \\ \hline 4,000 \end{array}$$

The answer should be about 4,000.

Add the ones.

$$\begin{array}{r} 2,803 \\ +\ 1,443 \\ \hline 6 \end{array}$$

As there are more than 10 hundreds, we change 10 hundreds to 1 thousand.

Add the tens.

$$\begin{array}{r} 2,803 \\ +\ 1,443 \\ \hline 46 \end{array}$$

Add the hundreds.

$$\begin{array}{r} {}^{1}2,803 \\ +\ 1,443 \\ \hline 246 \end{array}$$

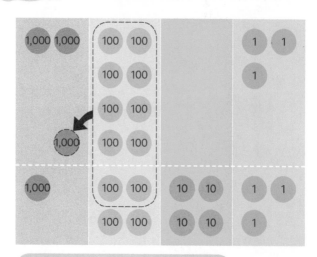

Add the thousands.

$$\begin{array}{r} {}^{1}2,803 \\ +\ 1,443 \\ \hline 4,246 \end{array}$$

Is the answer reasonable?

3. Find the value of
   (a) 1,028 + 234
   (b) 2,409 + 1,245
   (c) 4,190 + 649
   (d) 3,260 + 4,282
   (e) 6,204 + 993
   (f) 5,402 + 2,960

Exercise 14, pages 53—54

4. Find the sum of 1,266 and 2,355.

$$\begin{array}{r} 1,266 \\ +\ \ 2,355 \\ \hline \end{array}$$

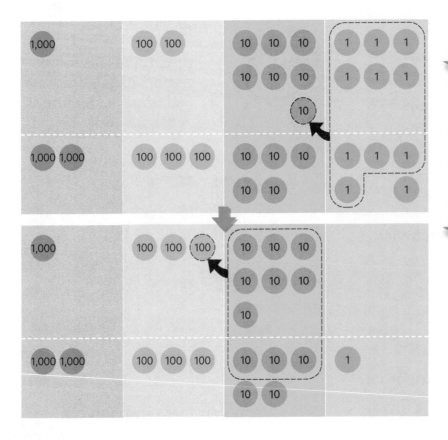

Add the ones.

$$\begin{array}{r} {}^{1} \\ 1,266 \\ +\ \ 2,355 \\ \hline 1 \end{array}$$

Add the tens.

$$\begin{array}{r} {}^{1}\ {}^{1} \\ 1,266 \\ +\ \ 2,355 \\ \hline 21 \end{array}$$

Add the hundreds.

$$\begin{array}{r} {}^{1}\ {}^{1} \\ 1,266 \\ +\ \ 2,355 \\ \hline 621 \end{array}$$

Add the thousands.

$$\begin{array}{r} {}^{1}\ {}^{1} \\ 1,266 \\ +\ \ 2,355 \\ \hline 3,621 \end{array}$$

5. Find the value of
   (a) 1,326 + 194
   (b) 3,762 + 5,158
   (c) 5,471 + 787
   (d) 6,942 + 1,095
   (e) 7,246 + 845
   (f) 4,653 + 2,729

6. Find the sum of 3,589 and 2,443.

$$\begin{array}{r} 3,589 \\ +\ 2,443 \\ \hline \end{array}$$

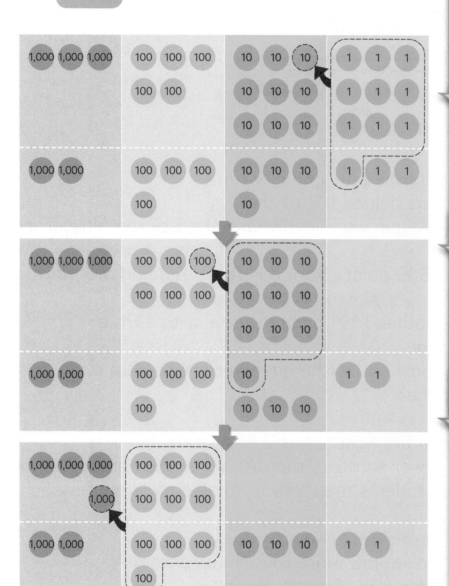

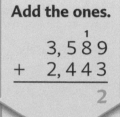

Add the ones.

$$\begin{array}{r} \overset{1}{} \\ 3,589 \\ +\ 2,443 \\ \hline 2 \end{array}$$

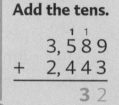

Add the tens.

$$\begin{array}{r} \overset{1}{\ }\overset{1}{\ } \\ 3,589 \\ +\ 2,443 \\ \hline 32 \end{array}$$

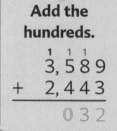

Add the hundreds.

$$\begin{array}{r} \overset{1}{\ }\overset{1}{\ }\overset{1}{\ } \\ 3,589 \\ +\ 2,443 \\ \hline 032 \end{array}$$

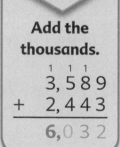

Add the thousands.

$$\begin{array}{r} \overset{1}{\ }\overset{1}{\ }\overset{1}{\ } \\ 3,589 \\ +\ 2,443 \\ \hline 6,032 \end{array}$$

7. Find the value of each of the following.
   Use estimation to see if your answers are reasonable.
   (a) 4,697 + 1,316   (b) 3,587 + 3,813
   (c) 2,908 + 5,892   (d) 2,824 + 2,576

8. Mr. Grey donated $3,745 to a charitable organization.
   Mr. Chen donated $2,861 more than Mr. Grey.
   How much did Mr. Chen donate?

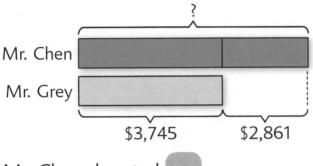

Mr. Chen donated ⬜ .

9. 2,583 people took part in a city run.
   314 volunteers helped out at the run.
   How many people were involved in the city run altogether?

10. Khun has 3,809 points from a library's reading program
    last year.
    He needs another 1,191 points this year to earn a
    reader's badge.
    How many points must he have in total to earn a
    reader's badge?

11. Irvine Elementary School has 2,374 students.
    It has 918 fewer students than Anaheim Elementary School.
    How many students are there in Anaheim Elementary School?

12. Factory A makes 3,937 toys.
    Factory B makes 165 more toys than Factory A.
    How many toys does Factory B make?

13. Larry spent $1,159 on a washing machine and has $1,905 left.
    How much money did he have at first?

Exercise 15, pages 55–56

6 Subtracting Ones, Tens, Hundreds, and Thousands

Subtract.

4,095 − 3 =

$$\begin{array}{r} 4{,}095 \\ -\phantom{4{,}09}3 \\ \hline \end{array}$$

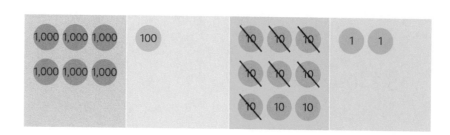

6,192 − 70 =

$$\begin{array}{r} 6{,}192 \\ -\phantom{6{,}1}70 \\ \hline \end{array}$$

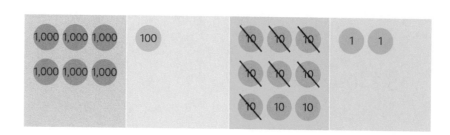

9,801 − 200 =

$$\begin{array}{r} 9{,}801 \\ -\phantom{9{,}}200 \\ \hline \end{array}$$

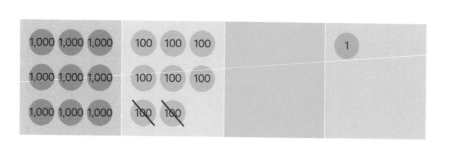

$8,793 - 5,000 =$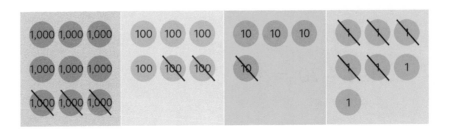

$$\begin{array}{r} 8,793 \\ -5,000 \\ \hline \end{array}$$

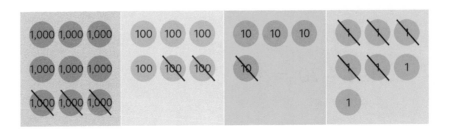

$9,647 - 3,215 =$

$$\begin{array}{r} 9,647 \\ -3,215 \\ \hline \end{array}$$

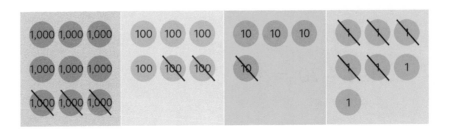

$5,340 - 6 =$

$$\begin{array}{r} 5,340 \\ -6 \\ \hline \end{array}$$

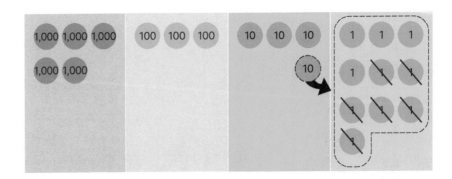

$4,500 - 80 = $ ⬜

$$
\begin{array}{r}
4,500 \\
-80 \\
\hline
\end{array}
$$ ⬜

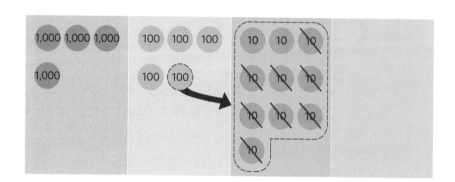

$7,000 - 300 = $ ⬜

$$
\begin{array}{r}
7,000 \\
-300 \\
\hline
\end{array}
$$ ⬜

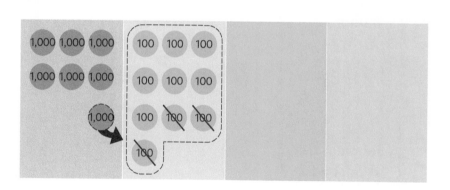

1. Find the value of
   (a) $6,847 - 3$ (b) $6,847 - 20$ (c) $6,847 - 500$
   (d) $6,847 - 4,000$ (e) $6,847 - 523$ (f) $6,847 - 4,523$

2. Find the value of
   (a) $3,760 - 2$ (b) $3,761 - 5$ (c) $5,402 - 40$
   (d) $5,442 - 60$ (e) $2,074 - 600$ (f) $2,274 - 700$

Exercise 16, pages 57–58

3. Find the difference between 3,246 and 1,634.

Subtract the ones.

$$\begin{array}{r} 3,246 \\ -\ 1,634 \\ \hline 2 \end{array}$$

Subtract the tens.

$$\begin{array}{r} 3,246 \\ -\ 1,634 \\ \hline 12 \end{array}$$

As there are not enough hundreds to subtract from, we change 1 thousand to 10 hundreds.

Subtract the hundreds.

$$\begin{array}{r} \overset{2\ \ 12}{3,\,\cancel{2}46} \\ -\ 1,634 \\ \hline 612 \end{array}$$

Subtract the thousands.

$$\begin{array}{r} \overset{2\ \ 12}{3,\,\cancel{2}46} \\ -\ 1,634 \\ \hline 1,612 \end{array}$$

$$\begin{array}{r} 3,246 \\ -\ 1,634 \\ \hline \end{array}$$

Check by adding.

$$\begin{array}{r} \\ +\ 1,634 \\ \hline 3,246 \end{array}$$

4. Find the value of
   (a) 4,821 − 514
   (b) 5,645 − 1,317
   (c) 6,743 − 461
   (d) 8,769 − 3,292
   (e) 9,674 − 853
   (f) 7,356 − 4,731

Exercise 17, pages 59–60

5. Find the difference between 2,435 and 1,268.

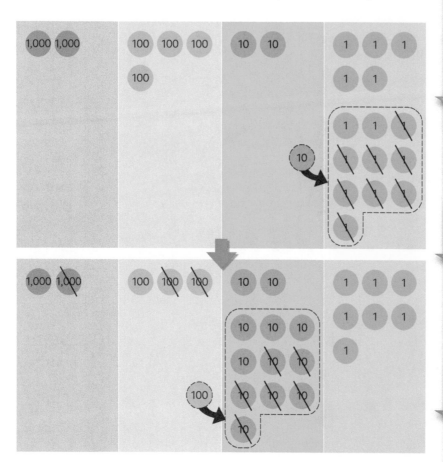

$$
\begin{array}{r}
2,435 \\
-\ 1,268 \\
\hline
\end{array}
$$

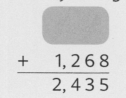

Check by adding.

$$
\begin{array}{r}
+\ 1,268 \\
\hline
2,435
\end{array}
$$

Subtract the ones.

$$
\begin{array}{r}
2,4\overset{2}{\cancel{3}}\overset{15}{\cancel{5}} \\
-\ 1,2\ 6\ 8 \\
\hline
7
\end{array}
$$

Subtract the tens.

$$
\begin{array}{r}
2,\overset{3}{\cancel{4}}\overset{12}{\cancel{3}}\overset{15}{\cancel{5}} \\
-\ 1,2\ 6\ 8 \\
\hline
6\ 7
\end{array}
$$

Subtract the hundreds.

$$
\begin{array}{r}
2,\overset{3}{\cancel{4}}\overset{12}{\cancel{3}}\overset{15}{\cancel{5}} \\
-\ 1,2\ 6\ 8 \\
\hline
1\ 6\ 7
\end{array}
$$

Subtract the thousands.

$$
\begin{array}{r}
2,\overset{3}{\cancel{4}}\overset{12}{\cancel{3}}\overset{15}{\cancel{5}} \\
-\ 1,2\ 6\ 8 \\
\hline
1,1\ 6\ 7
\end{array}
$$

6. Find the value of
   (a) 7,613 − 185
   (b) 8,450 − 4,262
   (c) 4,581 − 790
   (d) 9,608 − 6,894
   (e) 6,094 − 428
   (f) 3,640 − 1,807

7. Find the difference between 5,243 and 2,787.

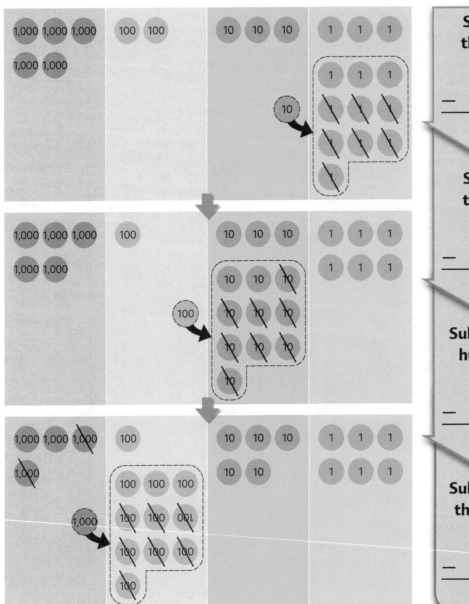

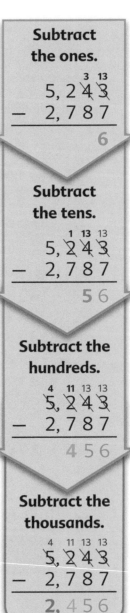

Subtract
the ones.

$$\begin{array}{r} \overset{3}{5},2\overset{13}{4}\cancel{3} \\ -\ 2,787 \\ \hline 6 \end{array}$$

Subtract
the tens.

$$\begin{array}{r} \overset{1}{5},\overset{13}{2}\overset{13}{4}\cancel{3} \\ -\ 2,787 \\ \hline 5\,6 \end{array}$$

Subtract the
hundreds.

$$\begin{array}{r} \overset{4}{5},\overset{11}{2}\overset{13}{4}\overset{13}{3} \\ -\ 2,787 \\ \hline 4\,5\,6 \end{array}$$

Subtract the
thousands.

$$\begin{array}{r} \overset{4}{5},\overset{11}{2}\overset{13}{4}\overset{13}{3} \\ -\ 2,787 \\ \hline 2,4\,5\,6 \end{array}$$

$$\begin{array}{r} 5,243 \\ -\ 2,787 \\ \hline \end{array}$$

Check by adding.

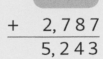

$$\begin{array}{r} +\ 2,787 \\ \hline 5,243 \end{array}$$

8. Find the value of each of the following.
   Use estimation to see if your answers are reasonable.
   (a) 9,564 − 8,467   (b) 6,875 − 3,996
   (c) 8,353 − 3,572   (d) 7,165 − 5,268

Exercise 18, pages 61–62

9. Find the difference between 6,000 and 257.

Change 1 thousand for 9 hundreds, 9 tens, and 10 ones.

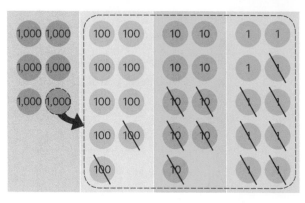

```
  6, 0 0 0
-    2 5 7
```
[ ]

Check by adding.

[ ]
```
+     2 5 7
   6, 0 0 0
```

Subtract the ones.
```
  5 9 9 10
  6, 0 0 0
-    2 5 7
          3
```

Subtract the tens.
```
  5 9 9 10
  6, 0 0 0
-    2 5 7
        4 3
```

Subtract the hundreds.
```
  5 9 9 10
  6, 0 0 0
-    2 5 7
      7 4 3
```

Subtract the thousands.
```
  5 9 9 10
  6, 0 0 0
-    2 5 7
   5, 7 4 3
```

10. 6,004 − 2,678 = [ ]

Subtract the ones.	**Subtract the tens.**	**Subtract the hundreds.**	**Subtract the thousands.**
5 9 9 14 6, 0 0 4 − 2, 6 7 8 6	5 9 9 14 6, 0 0 4 − 2, 6 7 8 2 6	5 9 9 14 6, 0 0 4 − 2, 6 7 8 3 2 6	5 9 9 14 6, 0 0 4 − 2, 6 7 8 3, 3 2 6

11. Find the value of
  (a) 4,000 − 392
  (b) 7,002 − 4,847
  (c) 3,020 − 2,430
  (d) 5,000 − 2,074

Check by adding.

[ ]
```
+   2, 6 7 8
    6, 0 0 4
```

12. Subtract.

5,200 − 948 =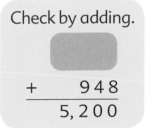

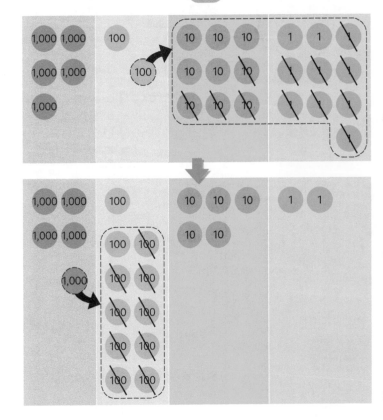

Subtract the ones.

$$\begin{array}{r} 5,\overset{1}{\cancel{2}}\overset{9}{\cancel{0}}\overset{10}{\cancel{0}} \\ -\quad 948 \\ \hline 2 \end{array}$$

Subtract the tens.

$$\begin{array}{r} 5,\overset{1}{\cancel{2}}\overset{9}{\cancel{0}}\overset{10}{\cancel{0}} \\ -\quad 948 \\ \hline 52 \end{array}$$

Subtract the hundreds.

$$\begin{array}{r} \overset{4}{\cancel{5}},\overset{11}{\cancel{2}}\overset{9}{\cancel{0}}\overset{10}{\cancel{0}} \\ -\quad 948 \\ \hline 252 \end{array}$$

Subtract the thousands.

$$\begin{array}{r} \overset{4}{\cancel{5}},\overset{11}{\cancel{2}}\overset{9}{\cancel{0}}\overset{10}{\cancel{0}} \\ -\quad 948 \\ \hline 4,252 \end{array}$$

$$\begin{array}{r} 5,200 \\ -\quad 948 \\ \hline \end{array}$$

Check by adding.

$$\begin{array}{r} \\ +\quad 948 \\ \hline 5,200 \end{array}$$

13. Find the value of
    (a) 8,007 − 3,429   (b) 6,900 − 745
    (c) 9,403 − 4,275   (d) 5,302 − 4,618
    (e) 4,025 − 1,387   (f) 4,100 − 1,432
    (g) 7,506 − 3,697   (h) 8,045 − 5,557
    (i) 9,205 − 6,749   (j) 6,300 − 4,451
    (k) 7,063 − 5,476   (l) 10,000 − 5,721

14. Ryan collected 4,945 used pens.
    He refilled some pens with ink and gave them away.
    He had 632 pens left.
    How many pens did he give away?

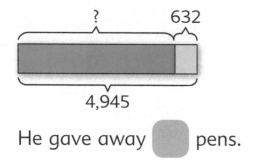

He gave away ___ pens.

15. Ms. Aniston spent $8,690 on a sofa set and $4,885 on a cupboard.
    How much more did she spend on the sofa set than on the cupboard?

16. 5,100 people took part in a story-writing camp over the weekend.
    2,638 of them were men and the rest were women.
    How many women took part in the story writing camp?

17. City Library has 6,021 books.
    Town Library has 2,508 fewer books than City Library.
    How many books does Town Library have?

18. John had $2,836. He had $1,048 left after buying a computer.
    How much did he spend on the computer?

19. There are 3,680 building blocks in Container A. There are 1,725 more building blocks in Container A than in Container B.
    How many building blocks are there in Container B?

Exercise 19, pages 63–64

7 Two-step Word Problems

Jamie picked 17 flowers.
Lindsey picked 12.
They gave away 20 of the flowers.
How many flowers were left?

Find the total number
of flowers they picked
altogether first.

$17 + 12 = 29$

They picked 29 flowers altogether.

$29 - 20 =$

 flowers were left.

1. Ali collected 137 stamps.
   He collected 27 fewer stamps than his sister.
   How many stamps did they collect altogether?

   $137 + 27 = a$

   $a =$

   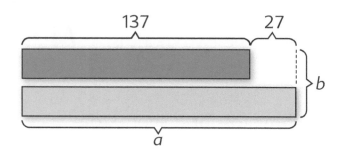

   Ali's sister collected 164 stamps.

   $137 + 164 = b$ $b =$

   They collected ⬜ stamps altogether.

2. 125 children took part in a mathematics competition.
   54 of them were girls.
   How many more boys than girls were there?

   $125 - 54 = 71$

   There were 71 boys.   Find the total number of boys first.

   $71 - 54 =$ ⬜

   There were ⬜ more boys than girls.

3. Kyle sold 337 boxes of cookies last month.
He sold 299 more boxes this month than last month.
How many boxes of cookies did he sell in the two months?

How many boxes of cookies did Kyle sell this month?

He sold boxes of cookies in the two months.

4. Eleanor and June wrote 1,805 words for a short story.
June wrote 873 words.
How many more words did Eleanor write?

How many words did Eleanor write?

Eleanor wrote more words.

5. There were 1,052 board books and picture books in a children's library.
650 of them were checked out.
226 of the books left were picture books.
How many board books were left?

What is the possible first step?

 board books were left.

6. Mitch bought 2,500 tiles.
   He used 1,164 tiles for one room and 940 tiles for
   another room.
   How many tiles were left?

7. Eric paid $628 for a television and $1,485 for a computer.
   He had $515 left.
   How much money did he have at first?

8. Tiffany saved $800.
   Melissa saved $204 less than Tiffany.
   Elvira saved $139 more than Melissa.
   How much did Elvira save?

Exercise 20, pages 65–67

1. $183 + n = 357$.
    What is the value of n that will make this equation true?

    (A) 174   (B) 234   (C) 430   (D) 540

2. 64 tens − 27 tens = _____.

    (A) 37   (B) 43   (C) 370   (D) 430

3. Select True or False.
    (a) $730 + 58 = 730 + 60 - 2$ True / False
    (b) $432 + 578 < 1,000$ True / False

4. Select True or False.
    (a) 8 ones + 45 ones = 8 tens + 45 tens   True / False
    (b) $6,009 - 137 = 6,009 - 140 + 3$ True / False

5. Find the value of
    (a) $1,730 + 313 = \boxed{}$ (b) $4,305 + \boxed{} = 6,484$

    (c) $\boxed{} + 3,161 = 8,426$

6. Find the value of
    (a) $8,746 - \boxed{} = 4,430$ (b) $\boxed{} - 2,187 = 3,123$

    (c) $2,600 - 782 = \boxed{}$

7. (a) Estimate the value of $469 + 37$ by rounding each
         number in the expression to the nearest ten.

    (b) Estimate the value of $4,598 - 432$ by rounding each
         number in the expression to the nearest hundred.

    (c) Estimate the value of $7,087 - 2,592$ by rounding each
         number in the expression to the nearest thousand.

Find the value of each of the following.
Use estimation to see if your answers are reasonable.

	(a)	(b)	(c)
8.	4,329 + 5,450	3,642 + 1,253	6,347 + 2,612
9.	7,465 − 3,214	5,796 − 2,264	8,677 − 5,312
10.	4,389 + 3,175	5,294 + 2,706	3,490 + 1,844
11.	7,804 − 6,935	8,000 − 3,405	3,378 − 2,499

12. The difference between two numbers is 48.
    The greater number is 126.
    What is the smaller number?

13. Mr. Ray paid $450 for a television set.
    He still had $450 left.
    How much money did he have at first?

14. A shop sold 957 beef burritos and 1,238 chicken burritos.
    How many burritos were sold altogether?
    What numbers should be put into the boxes below?

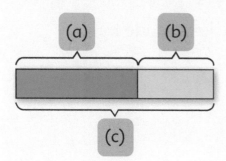

15. A total of 2,316 tickets were sold.
    1,548 tickets were for a football game.
    The rest were for a basketball game.
    How many tickets for the basketball game were sold?

16. 1,147 people went to the zoo by car.
    3,996 more people went to the zoo by bus than by car.
    How many people went to the zoo by bus?

17. The table shows the prices of two pianos.

Piano A	$2,005
Piano B	$1,542

How much cheaper is Piano B than Piano A?

18. Mrs. Marks earned $3,265.
Mrs. Spencer earned $2,955.
How much more money did Mrs. Marks earn than Mrs. Spencer?
What numbers should be in the boxes below?

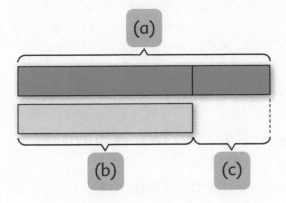

19. This table shows the number of crackers made by three machines in one hour.

Machine A	468
Machine B	652
Machine C	945

(a) What is the total number of crackers made by Machine A and Machine B?
(b) What is the total number of crackers made by the three machines?

20. Ryan had 35 tickets to sell.
He sold 15 tickets yesterday and 9 tickets today.
(a) How many tickets did he sell on the two days?
(b) How many tickets were not sold?

21. A farmer collected 1,930 chicken eggs.
    He collected 859 fewer duck eggs than chicken eggs.
    How many eggs did he collect altogether?

22. Ben made 1,050 peanut butter cookies and 950 oatmeal cookies.
    He sold all his cookies.
    Then he made 765 more cookies.
    How many cookies did he make altogether?

23. Mark earned $3,915.
    He spent $1,268 on food.
    He spent $1,380 on rent and transportation.
    How much did he have left?

24. Emily saved $1,035.
    Dorothy saved $278 more than Emily.
    Maria saved $105 less than Dorothy.
    How much did Maria save?

25. Miguel has 168 paper clips.
    Flora gives him 34 more.
    How many paper clips does Miguel have now?
    Which of the models below is more suitable for the
    word problem above? Explain your answer.

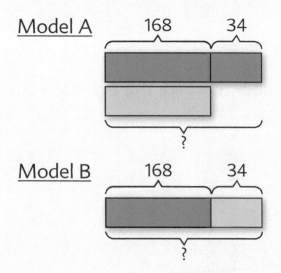

Model A   168   34

Model B   168   34

73

1. Which pair of numbers makes 1,000?
   (A) 456 and 443   (B) 621 and 489
   (C) 382 and 618   (D) 205 and 895

2. 400 tens − 281 tens = ☐ tens

   (A) 119   (B) 129   (C) 1,190   (D) 1,290

3. Select True or False.
   (a) $590 + 63 = 590 + 10 + 53$ True / False
   (b) 23 hundreds − 7 hundreds = 16   True / False

4. Select True or False.
   (a) $1,956 - 704 = 1,956 + 4 + 700$ True / False
   (b) $143 + 341 < 341 + 143$ True / False

5. Find the value of
   (a) ☐ $+ 1,184 = 3,908$ (b) $1,310 + 8,184 =$ ☐

   (c) $4,668 +$ ☐ $= 8,143$

6. Find the value of
   (a) $1,470 -$ ☐ $= 1,099$ (b) ☐ $- 4,298 = 2,329$

   (c) $2,004 - 1,385 =$ ☐

7. Replace each letter with a number to make the equation true.
   (a) $3,984 + 2,653 = n$ $n =$ ☐

   (b) $7,045 - 999 = n$ $n =$ ☐

   (c) $5,684 + n = 7,002$ $n =$ ☐

   (d) $6,032 - n = 1,532$ $n =$ ☐

Find the value of each of the following.
Use estimation to see if your answers are reasonable.

	(a)	(b)	(c)
8.	7,203 + 796	2,645 + 3,150	3,421 + 4,262
9.	5,475 − 4,451	4,978 − 1,927	9,657 − 5,313
10.	2,446 + 6,596	4,079 + 5,784	3,142 + 1,455
11.	7,042 − 5,170	9,000 − 6,571	7,173 − 3,654

12. A man bought 650 pastries for a party.
    There were 39 pastries left after the party.
    How many pastries were eaten during the party?

13. 429 concert tickets were sold on Sunday.
    64 more tickets were sold on Sunday than on Saturday.
    How many concert tickets were sold on Saturday?

14. There are 1,206 students in a school.
    47 of them were absent yesterday.
    How many students were present yesterday?

15. Alice saved $2,900.
    She saved $1,567 less than her brother.
    How much did her brother save?
    What numbers should be put into the boxes below?

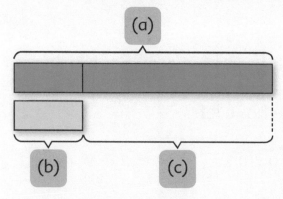

16. There were 2,055 men and 1,637 women at a concert.
    How many people were at the concert altogether?

17. $2,937 was donated by Mr. Garcia and Mr. Lin.
    Mr. Garcia donated $1,450.
    How much money did Mr. Lin donate?
    What numbers should be put into the boxes below?

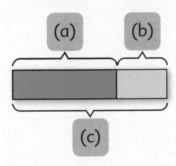

18. 1,730 people visited a book fair in the morning.
    2,545 people visited the book fair in the afternoon.
    How many more people visited the book fair in the afternoon
    than in the morning?

19. David collected 830 stamps.
    Peter collected 177 fewer stamps than David.
    (a) How many stamps did Peter collect?
    (b) How many stamps did they collect altogether?

20. In a school, there are 1,225 girls and 904 boys.
    (a) How many fewer boys are there than girls?
    (b) How many students are there altogether?

21. Mr. Johnson had $5,000.
    He spent $2,572 on a computer and $955 on a television set.
    (a) How much money did he spend?
    (b) How much money did he have left?

22. There are 4,608 members in a club.
    2,745 of them are men.
    855 are women.
    The rest are children.
    How many children are in the club?

23. A refrigerator costs $1,739.
    An oven is $850 cheaper than the refrigerator.
    Ms. Coles buys both the refrigerator and the oven.
    How much does she pay?

24. 4,100 children took part in an art competition.
    2,680 of them were boys.
    How many more boys than girls were there?

25. Mary had $2,467 in a bank.
    She deposited another $133.
    How much more money must she deposit if she wanted to have $3,000 in the bank?

26. Complete the table.

+	10	11	12	13	14	15	16	17	18	19	20
10	20	21	22	23	24	25	26	27	28	29	30
11	21	22	23	24	25	26	27	28			
12	22	23	24	25	26	27	28				
13	23	24	25	26	27	28					
14	24	25	26	27	28						
15	25	26	27	28							
16	26	27	28								
17	27	28									
18	28										
19	29										
20	30										

What pattern do you see in this addition table? Explain why the pattern works this way.

Review 2, pages 68–74

3 MULTIPLICATION AND DIVISION

1 Looking Back

2 multiplied by 4 is 8.
What is 2 multiplied by 5?

1. Complete the multiplication equations.

1 × 2 = 2	1 × 3 = 3	1 × 4 = 4
2 × 2 = 4	2 × 3 = 6	2 × 4 = 8
3 × 2 = 6	3 × 3 = 9	3 × 4 = 12
4 × 2 = ☐	4 × 3 = ☐	4 × 4 = ☐
5 × 2 = ☐	5 × 3 = ☐	5 × 4 = ☐
6 × 2 = ☐	6 × 3 = ☐	6 × 4 = ☐
7 × 2 = ☐	7 × 3 = ☐	7 × 4 = ☐
8 × 2 = ☐	8 × 3 = ☐	8 × 4 = ☐
9 × 2 = ☐	9 × 3 = ☐	9 × 4 = ☐
10 × 2 = ☐	10 × 3 = ☐	10 × 4 = ☐

1 × 5 = 5	1 × 10 = 10
2 × 5 = 10	2 × 10 = 20
3 × 5 = 15	3 × 10 = 30
4 × 5 = ☐	4 × 10 = ☐
5 × 5 = ☐	5 × 10 = ☐
6 × 5 = ☐	6 × 10 = ☐
7 × 5 = ☐	7 × 10 = ☐
8 × 5 = ☐	8 × 10 = ☐
9 × 5 = ☐	9 × 10 = ☐
10 × 5 = ☐	10 × 10 = ☐

2. Complete the equations.

(a)

$2 \times 5 = $ 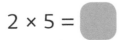 $5 \times 2 = $

(b)

$5 \times 2 = $ $2 \times 5 = $

$5 \times 2 = 2 + 2 + 2 + 2 + 2$ $2 \times 5 = 5 + 5$

Exercise 1, pages 75–77

3. Complete the equations.

$3 \times 4 = 4 \times $

$4 \times 3 = $ $3 \times 4 = $

$3 + 3 + 3 + 3 = $ $4 + 4 + 4 = $

4. How many stars are there on each pair of cards?

(a)

$3 \times 2 =$

(b)

$2 \times 2 =$

(c)

$1 \times 2 =$

(d)

$0 \times 2 =$

5. A player threw 3 rings over the post.
   For each ring that was thrown in, the player scored 2 points.
   How many points were scored in each of the following?

(a)

$2 \times 3 =$

(b)

$2 \times 2 =$

(c)

$2 \times 1 =$

(d)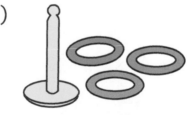

$2 \times 0 =$

6. Complete the equations.

$1 \times 0 = 0$ $3 \times 0 = 0$ $5 \times 0 = 0$

$2 \times 0 = $ $10 \times 0 = $ $100 \times 0 = $

Any number multiplied by 0 equals   .

7. Complete the equations.

$1 \times 1 = $ $2 \times 1 = $ $3 \times 1 = $

$1 \times 4 = $ $1 \times 10 = $ $100 \times 1 = $

Any number multiplied by 1 equals   .

8. Complete the equation.

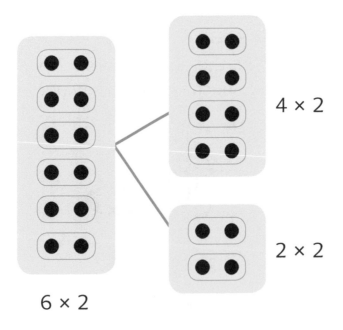

6×2

4×2

2×2

Find the value of the expression in the ( ) first.

$6 \times 2 = (4 \times 2) + (2 \times 2)$

$\quad\quad = \boxed{} + \boxed{}$

$\quad\quad = \boxed{}$

9. Complete the equation.

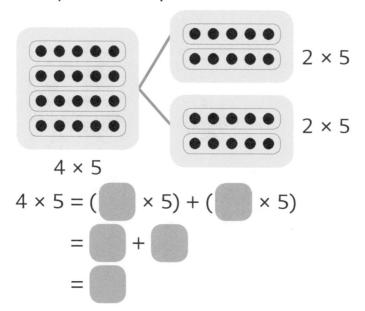

4 × 5

$4 \times 5 = (\boxed{} \times 5) + (\boxed{} \times 5)$

$= \boxed{} + \boxed{}$

$= \boxed{}$

10. Complete the equations.

(a) $8 \times 10 = (7 \times 10) + (\boxed{} \times 10)$

(b) $9 \times 3 = (5 \times 3) + (\boxed{} \times 3)$

(c) $(3 \times 2) + (4 \times 2) = (\boxed{} \times 2)$

(d) $(2 \times 5) + (4 \times 5) = (\boxed{} \times 5)$

Exercise 2, pages 78–81

11. There are 10 oranges.

(a) Divide 10 oranges equally into
     2 crates.
     How many oranges are there
     in each crate?

     $10 \div 2 = \boxed{}$

     There are $\boxed{}$ oranges in each crate.

(b) Divide 10 oranges into crates of 5. How many crates are
     there?

     $10 \div 5 = \boxed{}$

     There are $\boxed{}$ crates.

83

12. Complete the division equations.

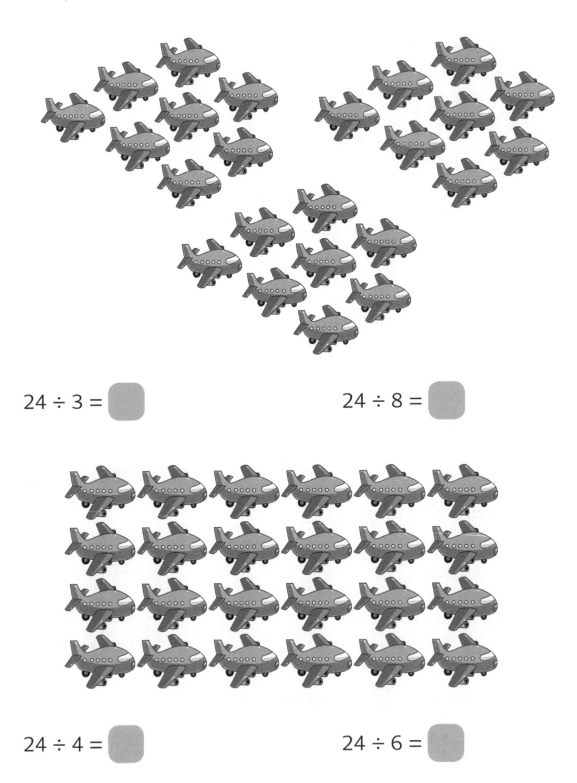

24 ÷ 3 = ☐

24 ÷ 8 = ☐

24 ÷ 4 = ☐

24 ÷ 6 = ☐

13. Complete the equations.

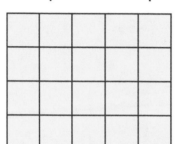

5 × 4 = ⬜

4 × 5 = ⬜

⬜ ÷ 4 = 5

⬜ ÷ 5 = 4

14. What are the missing numbers?

(a)
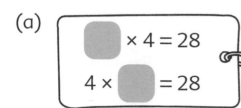

⬜ × 4 = 28

4 × ⬜ = 28

28 ÷ 4 = ⬜

(b)
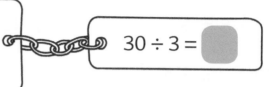

⬜ × 3 = 30

3 × ⬜ = 30

30 ÷ 3 = ⬜

(c)
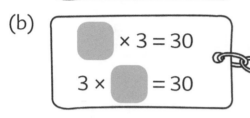

⬜ × 5 = 35

5 × ⬜ = 35

35 ÷ 5 = ⬜

(d)

⬜ × 10 = 40

10 × ⬜ = 40

40 ÷ 10 = ⬜

(e)
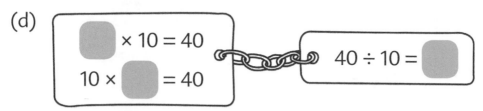

⬜ × 2 = 0

2 × ⬜ = 0

0 ÷ 2 = ⬜

(f)

⬜ × 10 = 10

10 × ⬜ = 10

10 ÷ 10 = ⬜

15. Complete the multiplication and division equations.

(a) $4 \times 7 = $ ▢

(b) $9 \times 3 = $ ▢

(c) $6 \times 3 = $ ▢

(d) $8 \times 2 = $ ▢

(e) $3 \times 7 = $ ▢

(f) $4 \times 6 = $ ▢

(g) $8 \times 5 = $ ▢

(h) $7 \times 2 = $ ▢

(i) $2 \times 6 = $ ▢

(j) $4 \times 4 = $ ▢

(k) $3 \times 10 = $ ▢

(l) $4 \times 5 = $ ▢

(m) $10 \times 8 = $ ▢

(n) $15 \div 3 = $ ▢

(o) $27 \div 3 = $ ▢

(p) $32 \div 4 = $ ▢

(q) $18 \div 3 = $ ▢

(r) $45 \div 5 = $ ▢

(s) $16 \div 2 = $ ▢

(t) $30 \div 3 = $ ▢

(u) $25 \div 5 = $ ▢

(v) $24 \div 4 = $ ▢

(w) $18 \div 2 = $ ▢

(x) $90 \div 10 = $ ▢

(y) $36 \div 4 = $ ▢

(z) $70 \div 10 = $ ▢

Exercise 3, pages 82–85

16. There were 24 chairs.
    18 of them were in 3 rows of 6.
    Mr. Gonzalez placed the rest of the chairs in another row of 6.

    (a) What symbol will make the following true?

    4 〇 6 = 24

    18 〇 6 = 24

    The total is 24.
    The symbol has to be + or ×.

    (b) What symbol will make the following true?

    24 〇 6 = 4

    24 〇 6 = 18

    The total is 24.
    The symbol has to be − or ÷.

17. Which sign goes in each 〇, **+, −, ×,** or **÷**?

    (a) 4 〇 4 = 16   (b) 4 〇 4 = 8

    (c) 12 〇 4 = 8   (d) 12 〇 3 = 4

    (e) 13 〇 7 = 2 × 3   (f) 6 × 4 = 8 〇 3

18. Which sign goes in each 〇, **>, <,** or **=**?

    (a) 3 × 4 〇 4 × 3   (b) 2 × 6 〇 6 × 3

    (c) 35 ÷ 5 〇 40 ÷ 4   (d) 5 × 8 〇 35 + 5

    (e) 3 × 6 〇 2 × 9   (f) 24 ÷ 3 〇 3 × 4

Exercise 4, pages 86–88

19. There are 8 buttons on each card.
How many buttons are there on 5 cards?

Multiply 8 by 5.

8 × 5 = ▢

There are ▢ buttons altogether.

20. Nicole ate 3 bowls of strawberries.
There were 8 strawberries in each bowl.
How many strawberries did she eat altogether?

3 × 8 = ▢

Nicole ate ▢ strawberries altogether.

21. A tailor used 21 m of cloth to make dresses.
She used 3 m of cloth for each dress.
How many dresses did she make?

21 ÷ 3 = ▢

3 × ▢ = 21

21 ÷ 3 = ▢

She made ▢ dresses.

22. Sean arranged 24 toy cars in 4 rows.
    There were an equal number of toy cars in each row.
    How many toy cars were there in each row?

    24 ÷ 4 = ⬜

    There were ⬜ toy cars in each row.

23. For each word problem, state whether you multiply or divide.
    Then solve the problem.

    (a) Denise saved $5 a week for 8 weeks.
        How much did she save altogether?

    (b) Ashley paid $18 for 3 shirts.
        What was the cost of 1 shirt?

    (c) Wendy baked 6 cakes.
        She put 10 cherries on each cake.
        How many cherries did she use altogether?

    (d) David bought 4 pineapples at $3 each.
        How much did he pay altogether?

    (e) There were 27 desks to clean.
        3 boys shared the work equally.
        How many desks did each boy clean?

    (f) 3 children made 24 birthday cards altogether.
        Each child made the same number of cards.
        How many cards did each child make?

Exercise 5, pages 89—90

2 More Word Problems

There are 9 blue flowers.
There are 3 times as many red flowers as blue flowers.
How many red flowers are there?

There are more red flowers than blue flowers.

Multiply 9 by 3.

9

9 × 3

9 × 3 = 27

There are ⬜ red flowers.

1. Melanie has $16.
   She has twice as much money as Sally.
   How much money does Sally have?

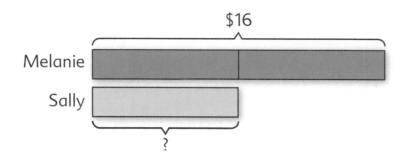

Divide 16 by 2.

16 ÷ 2 = ☐

Sally has $ ☐ .

2. 4 children bought a present for $28.
   They shared the cost equally.
   How much did each child pay?

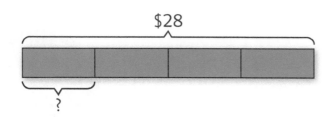

28 ÷ 4 = ☐

Each child paid $ ☐ .

4 units = $28
1 unit = $28 ÷ 4

3. 5 children shared the cost of a book equally.
   Each of them paid $6.
   What was the cost of the book?

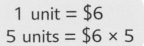

1 unit = $6
5 units = $6 × 5

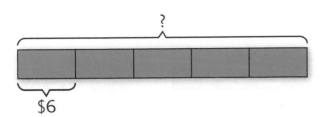

?

$6

$6 × 5 = ⬜

The cost of the book was $⬜.

Exercise 6, pages 91–93

4. A farmer has 7 ducks.
   He has 5 times as many chickens as ducks.
   How many more chickens than ducks does he have?

Find the number
of chickens first.

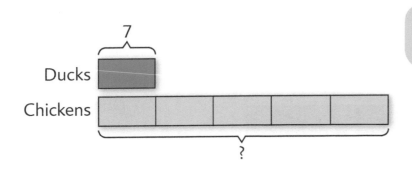

7

Ducks

Chickens

?

7 × 5 = 35

He has 35 chickens.

35 − 7 = ⬜

He has ⬜ more chickens than ducks.

5. Mary bought 3 dresses.
   Each dress cost $8.
   She gave the cashier $30.
   How much change did she get back?

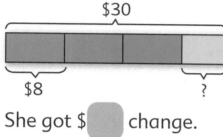

   She got $☐ change.

6. Li Wei has 5 color pencils.
   Mavis has 3 times as many color pencils as Li Wei.
   How many color pencils do they have altogether?

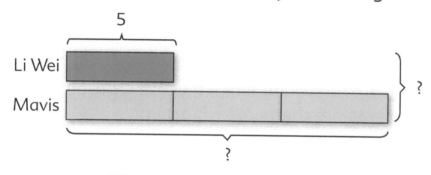

   Mavis has ☐ color pencils.

   They have ☐ color pencils altogether.

7. Sam spent $32 on 4 toy cars and a toy airplane.
   The airplane cost $12.
   How much more did the airplane cost than 1 toy car?

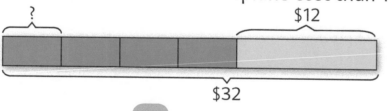

   1 toy car cost $☐.

   The airplane cost $☐ more than 1 toy car.

8. Peter has $12.
   He has twice as much money as Paul.
   John has $2 less than Paul.
   How much money does John have?

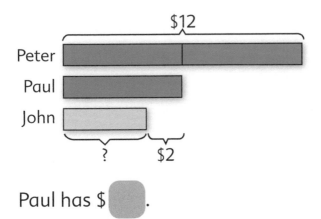

Paul has $ ☐.

John has $ ☐.

9. There are 16 boys and 12 girls.
   Mr. Denzel puts all the students equally into 4 groups.
   How many students are there in each group?

   There are ☐ students in each group.

10. Grace has 6 badges.
    Quinn has 4 more badges than Grace.
    Amanda has 2 times as many badges as Quinn.
    How many badges does Amanda have?

    Quinn has ☐ badges.

    Amanda has ☐ badges.

Solve the problems.

11. Andy earned $10 a day.
    He worked for 7 days.
    How much did he earn altogether?

12. Harry has $36.
    He has 4 times as much money as his brother.
    How much money does his brother have?

13. Devi practiced the piano for 2 hours each day.
    How many hours did she practice in 8 days?

14. Lynn had 16 flowers.
    She put 4 flowers into each vase.
    How many vases did she use?

15. Miss Levinsky graded 5 sets of 8 journals in the morning.
    She graded 30 journals in the afternoon.
    (a) How many journals did she grade in the morning?
    (b) How many journals did she grade altogether?

16. There are 27 red balloons.
    There are 3 times as many red balloons as blue balloons.
    How many balloons are there altogether?

17. Ryan bought 18 pencils.
    He bought twice as many pencils as pens.
    How much did he pay for the pens if each pen cost $3?

18. Brian has 6 goldfish.
    He has 5 times as many guppies as goldfish.
    If he puts 3 guppies into each tank, how many
    tanks does he need?

19. Emily bought 4 boxes of pencils.
    Each box has an equal number of pencils.
    There were 32 pencils altogether.
    There were 5 blue pencils and some red pencils
    in each box.
    How many red pencils were there in each box?

3 Multiplying Ones, Tens, and Hundreds

1 1 1 1
1 1 1 1
1 1 1 1

4 × 3 = 12

Multiply 4 ones by 3:
4 ones × 3 = 12 ones

10 10 10 10
10 10 10 10
10 10 10 10

40 × 3 = ☐

Multiply 4 tens by 3:
4 tens × 3 = 12 tens

100 100 100 100
100 100 100 100
100 100 100 100

400 × 3 = ☐

Multiply 4 hundreds by 3:
4 hundreds × 3 = 12 hundreds

4 × 3 = 12	40 × 3 = 120	400 × 3 = 1,200

$$4 \times 3 = 12$$
$$\begin{array}{r} 4 \\ \times\ 3 \\ \hline 12 \end{array}$$

12 ones

$$40 \times 3 = 120$$
$$\begin{array}{r} 4\mathbf{0} \\ \times\ \ 3 \\ \hline 12\mathbf{0} \end{array}$$

12 tens

$$400 \times 3 = 1{,}200$$
$$\begin{array}{r} 4\mathbf{00} \\ \times\ \ \ 3 \\ \hline 1{,}2\mathbf{00} \end{array}$$

12 hundreds

1. Find the value of
    (a) 9 × 5   (b) 90 × 5   (c) 900 × 5
    (d) 5 × 9   (e) 50 × 9   (f) 500 × 9
    (g) 6 × 5   (h) 60 × 5   (i) 600 × 5
    (j) 20 × 3   (k) 200 × 3   (l) 2,000 × 3

2. A bookseller sold 30 books on the first day.
    On the second day, he sold 8 times as many books as
    on the first day.
    How many books did he sell on the second day?

3 tens × 8 = ☐ tens

30 × 8 = ☐

He sold ☐ books on the second day.

3. Find the value of
    (a) 20 × 9   (b) 90 × 2
    (c) 4 × 500   (d) 400 × 5
    (e) 40 × 6   (f) 5 × 10
    (g) 800 × 5   (h) 4 × 400
    (i) 50 × 2   (j) 4 × 30
    (k) 100 × 8   (l) 70 × 3
    (m) 30 × 9   (n) 3 × 10
    (o) 30 × 10   (p) 300 × 10

Exercise 8, pages 97–98

4. Multiply 12 by 4.

$$
\begin{array}{r}
1\,2 \\
\times \quad 4 \\
\hline
\end{array}
$$

10 × 4 = 40   2 × 4 = 8

Multiply the ones by 4.

$$
\begin{array}{r}
1\,2 \\
\times \quad 4 \\
\hline
8
\end{array}
$$

Multiply the tens by 4.

$$
\begin{array}{r}
1\,2 \\
\times \quad 4 \\
\hline
4\,8
\end{array}
$$

12 × 4 = (**10** × 4) + (**2** × 4)
= 40 + 8

When we multiply 12 by 4, the **product** is 48.

5. Find the product.
    (a) 23 × 3   (b) 32 × 2   (c) 2 × 42   (d) 4 × 21

6. Multiply 42 by 3.

$$
\begin{array}{r}
4\,2 \\
\times \quad 3 \\
\hline
\end{array}
$$

4 0
2 × 3

42 × 3 = (**40** × 3) + (**2** × 3)
= 120 + 6

Multiply the ones by 3.

$$
\begin{array}{r}
4\,2 \\
\times \quad 3 \\
\hline
6
\end{array}
$$

Multiply the tens by 3.

$$
\begin{array}{r}
4\,2 \\
\times \quad 3 \\
\hline
1\,2\,6
\end{array}
$$

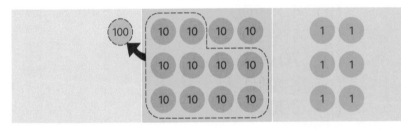

7. Find the product.
    (a) 52 × 3   (b) 64 × 2   (c) 91 × 4   (d) 73 × 2

Exercise 9, pages 99–100

8. Multiply 24 by 3.

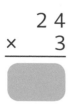

$$24 \times 3 = (20 \times 3) + (4 \times 3)$$
$$= 60 + 12$$

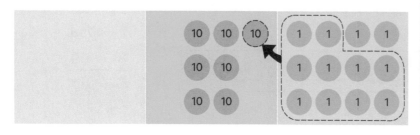

Multiply the ones by 3.

$$\overset{1}{2}4$$
$$\times \quad 3$$
$$\overline{2}$$

Multiply the tens by 3.

$$\overset{1}{2}4$$
$$\times \quad 3$$
$$\overline{7\,2}$$

9. Find the product.
    (a) 17 × 4   (b) 26 × 3   (c) 38 × 2   (d) 19 × 5

10. Multiply 34 by 3.

$$34 \times 3 = (30 \times 3) + (4 \times 3)$$
$$= 90 + 12$$

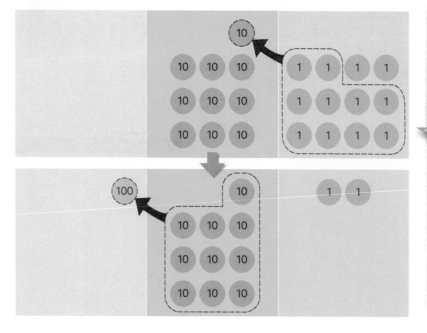

Multiply the ones by 3.

$$\overset{1}{3}4$$
$$\times \quad 3$$
$$\overline{2}$$

Multiply the tens by 3.

$$\overset{1}{3}4$$
$$\times \quad 3$$
$$\overline{10\,2}$$

11. Find the product.
    (a) 81 × 2   (b) 16 × 3   (c) 3 × 37
    (d) 52 × 4   (e) 23 × 4   (f) 5 × 45
    (g) 63 × 3   (h) 24 × 5   (i) 4 × 38

12. Melvin had 4 baskets of strawberries.
    He had 24 strawberries in each basket.
    How many strawberries did he have altogether?

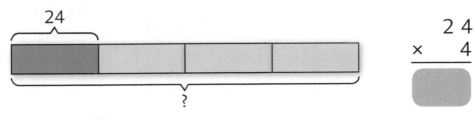

$$\begin{array}{r} 2\,4 \\ \times\ \ \ 4 \\ \hline \end{array}$$

He had ⬜ strawberries altogether.

13. There are 5 rows of tiles.
    There are 56 tiles in each row.
    How many tiles are there altogether?

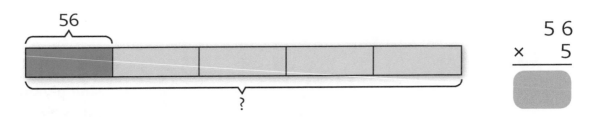

$$\begin{array}{r} 5\,6 \\ \times\ \ \ 5 \\ \hline \end{array}$$

There are ⬜ tiles altogether.

Exercise 10, pages 101–103

100

14. Fill in the missing numbers.

$3 \times 342 = $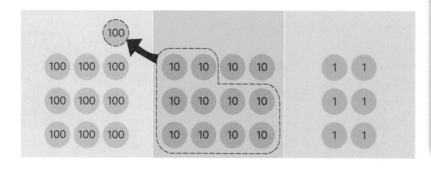

$$
\begin{array}{r}
3\,4\,2 \\
\times\ \ \ \ \ 3 \\
\hline
\end{array}
$$

```
3 0 0
  4 0    × 3
    2
```

$342 \times 3 = (300 \times 3) + (40 \times 3) + (2 \times 3)$
$= 900 + 120 + 6$

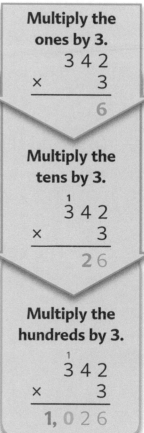

Multiply the ones by 3.
$$
\begin{array}{r}
3\,4\,2 \\
\times\ \ \ \ \ 3 \\
\hline
6
\end{array}
$$

Multiply the tens by 3.
$$
\begin{array}{r}
\overset{1}{3}\,4\,2 \\
\times\ \ \ \ \ 3 \\
\hline
2\,6
\end{array}
$$

Multiply the hundreds by 3.
$$
\begin{array}{r}
\overset{1}{3}\,4\,2 \\
\times\ \ \ \ \ 3 \\
\hline
1,\!0\,2\,6
\end{array}
$$

15. Find the product of 245 and 3.

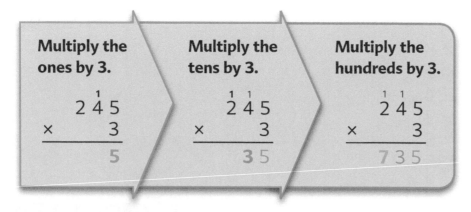

Multiply the ones by 3.
$$
\begin{array}{r}
2\,\overset{1}{4}\,5 \\
\times\ \ \ \ \ 3 \\
\hline
5
\end{array}
$$

Multiply the tens by 3.
$$
\begin{array}{r}
\overset{1}{2}\,\overset{1}{4}\,5 \\
\times\ \ \ \ \ 3 \\
\hline
3\,5
\end{array}
$$

Multiply the hundreds by 3.
$$
\begin{array}{r}
\overset{1}{2}\,\overset{1}{4}\,5 \\
\times\ \ \ \ \ 3 \\
\hline
7\,3\,5
\end{array}
$$

$245 \times 3 = $

16. (a) Estimate the value of 212 × 4.

200 × 4 =

The value of 212 × 4 is about .

212 is 200 rounded to the nearest hundred.

(b) Find the value of 212 × 4.

212 × 4 = ⬜

The value of 212 × 4 is ⬜.

```
    2 1 2
  ×     4
  ───────
    8 4 8
```

848 is close to 800.
The answer is reasonable.

17. Find the product for each of the following.
    Use estimation to see if your answer is reasonable.
    (a) 214 × 2
    (b) 323 × 3
    (c) 4 × 231
    (d) 620 × 3
    (e) 451 × 2
    (f) 3 × 234
    (g) 289 × 3
    (h) 704 × 5
    (i) 5 × 436

Exercise 11, pages 104—105

18. There are 950 staples in a box.
    How many staples are there in 3 such boxes?

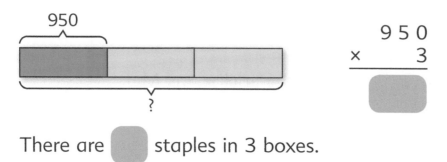

    There are [ ] staples in 3 boxes.

19. Drew has $598.
    Connie has 4 times as much money as Drew.

    (a) About how much money does Connie have?

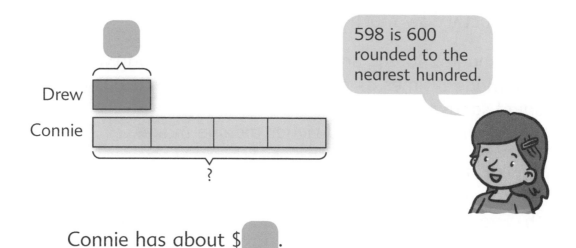

598 is 600 rounded to the nearest hundred.

    Connie has about $[ ].

    (b) Exactly how much money does Connie have?

    Connie has $[ ].

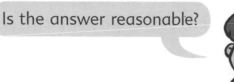

Is the answer reasonable?

Solve the problems.

20. There are 52 weeks in a year.
How many weeks are there in 4 years?

21. Mel collected 76 stickers.
Sue collected 3 times as many stickers as Mel.
How many stickers did Sue collect?

22. A refrigerator costs 5 times as much as a microwave oven.
The microwave costs $259.
What is the total cost of the refrigerator and the microwave?

23. A radio costs $262.
A television costs 4 times as much as the radio.
(a) About how much does the television cost?
(b) Exactly how much does the television cost?

24. Kate made 280 egg salad sandwiches for a party.
She made 3 times as many chicken sandwiches as egg salad sandwiches.
How many chicken sandwiches did she make?

25. A pilot flies 850 hours in one month.
(a) About how many hours will he fly in 5 months?
(b) Exactly how many hours will he fly in 5 months?

26. There are 18 chairs in the first row.
There are 25 chairs in each of the other 5 rows.
How many chairs are there altogether?

27. There were 30 cakes in one box.
Wendy bought 4 such boxes of cakes.
How much did she pay for the cakes if each cake cost $3?

28. Cassey sold 680 eggs last week.
She sold 4 times as many eggs this week as last week.
How many eggs did she sell altogether?

Exercise 12, pages 106–107

4 Quotient and Remainder

Chris has 14 books.
He puts the books equally onto 4 shelves.
How many books are there on each shelf?
How many books are left over?

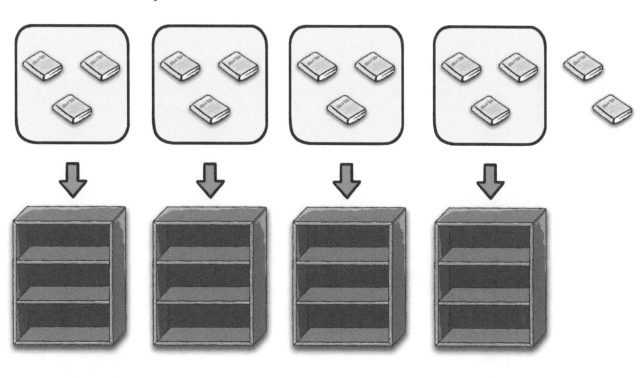

We write:
$14 \div 4 = 3$ R 2

$14 \div 4 = 3$ with a remainder of 2

There are ⬜ books on each shelf.

⬜ books are left over.

$$\begin{array}{r} 3\,R\,2 \\ 4\overline{)\,14} \\ 12 \\ \hline 2 \end{array}$$

3×4

$14 - 12$

When 14 is divided by 4, the **quotient** is 3 and the **remainder** is 2.
We write the answer as 3 **R** 2.

Check your answer.

Quotient × 4 = 3 × 4 = 12

12 + remainder = 12 + 2 = **14**

Is 14 the number we divided?

1. Divide 9 by 2.

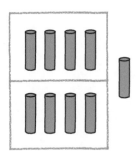

$$\begin{array}{r} 4\,R\,1 \\ 2\overline{)\,9} \\ 8 \\ \hline 1 \end{array}$$

9 ÷ 2 = ⬜

4 × 2 = 8

8 + 1 = ⬜

2. Divide 12 by 2.

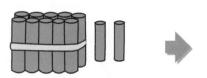

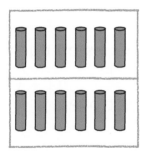

$$\begin{array}{r} 6 \\ 2\overline{)\,12} \\ 12 \\ \hline 0 \end{array}$$

12 ÷ 2 = ⬜

6 × 2 = 12

12 + 0 = ⬜

3. Divide.

$28 \div 2 =$

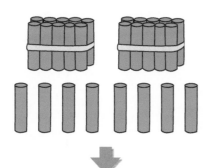

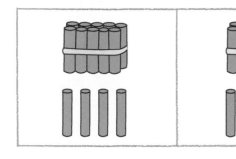

4. Divide.

$34 \div 2 =$

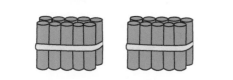

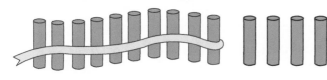

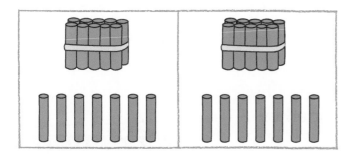

5. Divide.

$73 \div 2 = \boxed{}$

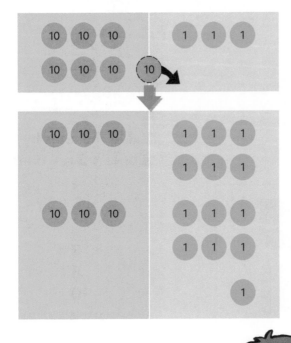

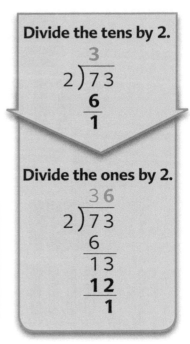

Divide the tens by 2.

$$\begin{array}{r} 3 \\ 2)\overline{73} \\ \underline{6} \\ 1 \end{array}$$

Divide the ones by 2.

$$\begin{array}{r} 36 \\ 2)\overline{73} \\ \underline{6} \\ 13 \\ \underline{12} \\ 1 \end{array}$$

$$\begin{array}{r} 36\,\text{R}\,1 \\ 2)\overline{73} \\ \underline{6} \\ 13 \\ \underline{12} \\ 1 \end{array}$$

When 73 is divided by 2, the quotient is $\boxed{}$

and the remainder is $\boxed{}$.

6.

> Numbers in which the ones digit is **0, 2, 4, 6,** or **8** are called **even numbers**.
> Numbers in which the ones digit is **1, 3, 5, 7,** or **9** are called **odd numbers**.

What can you say about the remainder in each of the following?

(a) An even number divided by 2
(b) An odd number divided by 2

Exercise 13, pages 108–109

7. Divide.

$96 \div 4 = $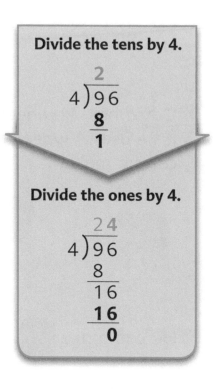

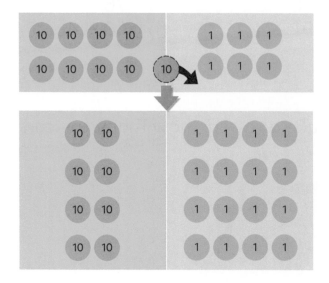

When 96 is divided by 4,

the quotient is ___ and the

remainder is ___ .

Divide the tens by 4.

$$
\begin{array}{r}
2 \\
4\overline{)96} \\
\underline{8} \\
1
\end{array}
$$

Divide the ones by 4.

$$
\begin{array}{r}
24 \\
4\overline{)96} \\
\underline{8} \\
16 \\
\underline{16} \\
0
\end{array}
$$

8. Divide.

$80 \div 3 = $ ___

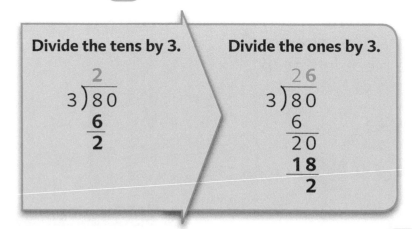

Divide the tens by 3.

$$
\begin{array}{r}
2 \\
3\overline{)80} \\
\underline{6} \\
2
\end{array}
$$

Divide the ones by 3.

$$
\begin{array}{r}
26 \\
3\overline{)80} \\
\underline{6} \\
20 \\
\underline{18} \\
2
\end{array}
$$

When 80 is divided by 3, the quotient is ___ and the

remainder is ___ .

9. Find the quotient and remainder for each of the following:
   (a) 48 ÷ 2   (b) 60 ÷ 3   (c) 54 ÷ 3
   (d) 51 ÷ 4   (e) 75 ÷ 5   (f) 67 ÷ 5
   (g) 82 ÷ 2   (h) 58 ÷ 3   (i) 76 ÷ 1
   (j) 80 ÷ 5   (k) 91 ÷ 4   (l) 60 ÷ 4

10. David has 74 wheels.
    If he uses 4 wheels to make a toy car, how many toy cars
    can he make?

4)74

He can make toy cars.

 wheels are left over.

11. Justine has 89 m of wire.
    She cuts it into shorter pieces.
    Each piece is 3 m long.
    How many pieces does she have?
    How long is the piece left over?

    She has ▢ pieces.

    The left over piece is ▢ m long.

Exercise 14, pages 110–111

5 Dividing Hundreds, Tens, and Ones

Divide.

$400 \div 2 = $

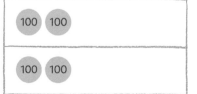

4 hundreds ÷ 2

$500 \div 2 = $

5 hundreds ÷ 2

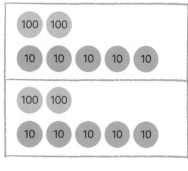

$550 \div 2 = $

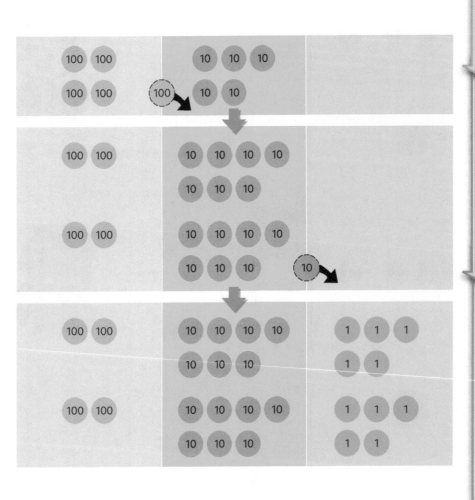

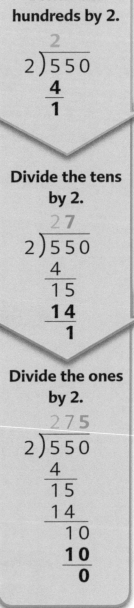

1. Divide.

   426 ÷ 3 = ◻

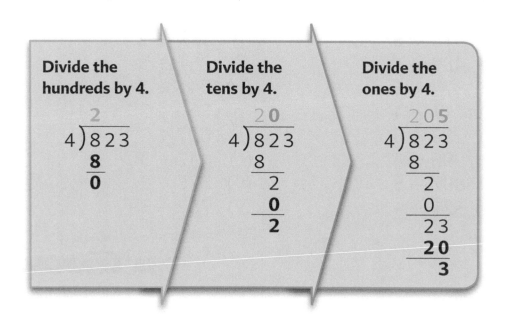

Divide the hundreds by 3.	Divide the tens by 3.	Divide the ones by 3.

2. Divide.

   823 ÷ 4 = ◻

Divide the hundreds by 4.	Divide the tens by 4.	Divide the ones by 4.

3. Divide.

$237 \div 5 = \boxed{}$

Divide the hundreds by 5.	Divide the tens by 5.	Divide the ones by 5.
$\begin{array}{r} 0 \\ 5\overline{)237} \\ \underline{0} \\ 2 \end{array}$	$\begin{array}{r} 04 \\ 5\overline{)237} \\ \underline{0} \\ 23 \\ \underline{20} \\ 3 \end{array}$	$\begin{array}{r} 047 \\ 5\overline{)237} \\ \underline{0} \\ 23 \\ \underline{20} \\ 37 \\ \underline{35} \\ 2 \end{array}$

4. Find the quotient and remainder for each of the following:
   (a) $352 \div 4$ (b) $640 \div 2$
   (c) $433 \div 5$ (d) $700 \div 3$
   (e) $290 \div 4$ (f) $105 \div 3$
   (g) $249 \div 4$ (h) $374 \div 2$
   (i) $511 \div 5$ (j) $163 \div 2$
   (k) $489 \div 4$ (l) $251 \div 3$
   (m) $374 \div 5$ (n) $547 \div 2$
   (o) $719 \div 4$ (p) $860 \div 3$
   (q) $288 \div 5$ (r) $607 \div 2$
   (s) $995 \div 4$ (t) $442 \div 3$
   (u) $897 \div 5$ (v) $575 \div 2$
   (w) $321 \div 4$ (x) $787 \div 3$

Exercise 15, pages 112–113

5. Complete the equations.

(a) $6 \div 3 = \boxed{}$

$(\ 1 \ \ 1 \ )$ $(\ 1 \ \ 1 \ )$ $(\ 1 \ \ 1 \ )$

6 ones $\div$ 3 = $\boxed{}$ ones

(b) $60 \div 3 = \boxed{}$

$(\ 10 \ \ 10 \ )$ $(\ 10 \ \ 10 \ )$ $(\ 10 \ \ 10 \ )$

6 tens $\div$ 3 = $\boxed{}$ tens

(c) $600 \div 3 = \boxed{}$

$(\ 100 \ \ 100 \ )$ $(\ 100 \ \ 100 \ )$ $(\ 100 \ \ 100 \ )$

6 hundreds $\div$ 3 = $\boxed{}$ hundreds

(d) $6{,}000 \div 3 = \boxed{}$

$(\ 1{,}000 \ \ 1{,}000 \ )$ $(\ 1{,}000 \ \ 1{,}000 \ )$ $(\ 1{,}000 \ \ 1{,}000 \ )$

6 thousands $\div$ 3 = $\boxed{}$ thousands

6. Complete the equations.

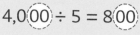
4,000 ÷ 5 = 800

$40 \div 5 = \boxed{}$

$400 \div 5 = \boxed{}$

$4{,}000 \div 5 = \boxed{}$

7. Divide.
   (a) $9 \div 3$ (b) $90 \div 3$ (c) $900 \div 3$
   (d) $40 \div 2$ (e) $360 \div 4$ (f) $400 \div 5$
   (g) $320 \div 4$ (h) $2{,}400 \div 4$ (i) $1{,}000 \div 5$

8. Estimate the value of 167 ÷ 3.

180 ÷ 3 =

200 ÷ 3 = ?

I can't round to the nearest hundred.
There will be a remainder.

167 ⟨ 150 ÷ 3
       180 ÷ 3

The value of 167 ÷ 3 is about .

9. Ashley made 276 muffins.
    She put them into boxes of 4 muffins each.
    How many boxes of muffins were there?
    How many were left over?

    (a) Estimate the number of boxes.

276 ÷ 4 = ?
4 × 6 = 24
4 × 7 = 28
I will use 280.

280 ÷ 4 =

The answer will be around 70.

    (b) Find the answer.

There were boxes of muffins.

 muffins were left over.

10. Estimate the value of
    (a) 842 ÷ 4
    (b) 378 ÷ 2
    (c) 98 ÷ 5
    (d) 568 ÷ 3
    (e) 512 ÷ 2
    (f) 1,693 ÷ 4

11. 5 bicycles cost $750.
    How much does one bicycle cost?

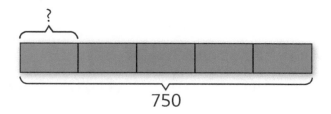

750

1 bicycle costs .

12. Craig has 317 oranges.
    He puts 3 oranges in each bag.
    How many bags of oranges can he make?
    How many oranges will be left over?

    He can make ⬜ bags of oranges.

    ⬜ oranges will be left over.

Exercise 16, pages 114—115

REVIEW 3

1. What is the value of 4 × 5?
   (A) 9   (B) 20   (C) 45   (D) 54

2. What is the product of 7 tens and 3?
   (A) 10   (B) 21   (C) 73   (D) 210

3. What is the quotient of 378 ÷ 4?
   (A) 2   (B) 94   (C) 374   (D) 1,512

4. What is the remainder when 627 is divided by 3?
   (A) 1   (B) 2   (C) 3   (D) 0

5. A number is divided by 5. The quotient is 9 and the remainder is 2.
   What is the number?
   (A) 16   (B) 19   (C) 43   (D) 47

6. Select True or False.
   (a) 8 × 5 > 5 × 8   True / False
   (b) 3 + 3 + 3 = 3 × 3   True / False
   (c) 5 × 0 = 0 × 20   True / False
   (d) 24 ÷ 6 = 24 ÷ 4   True / False

7. Select True or False.
   (a) 9 × 4 = 7 × 4 + 2 × 4   True / False
   (b) 6 × 3 + 2 × 3 = 7 × 3   True / False
   (c) 6 tens × 2 = 120   True / False
   (d) 4 hundreds × 4 = 16   True / False

8. Find the value of
   (a) 15 × 1   (b) 1 × 99   (c) 9 × 0
   (d) 0 × 7   (e) 0 ÷ 6   (f) 8 ÷ 8

9. Which sign goes in each ⬤, >, < or =?
   (a) 4 × 7 ⬤ 24 + 7   (b) 4,395 × 0 ⬤ 0 ÷ 5

   (c) 345 × 1 ⬤ 1 × 354   (d) 4 × 35 ⬤ 35 × 5

   (e) 105 ÷ 5 ⬤ 21 × 5   (f) 4,562 + 1,438 ⬤ 1,200 × 4

10. Which sign goes in each ⬤, +, −, × or ÷?
    (a) 28 ⬤ 4 = 7   (b) 45 ⬤ 5 = 40

    (c) 36 ⬤ 3 = 108   (d) 82 ⬤ 2 = 41

    (e) 10 ⬤ 0 = 0   (f) 600 ⬤ 3 = 1,800

11. Estimate the value of
    (a) 378 × 4   (b) 3 × 973
    (c) 329 ÷ 4   (d) 193 ÷ 3

Find the value of

	(a)	(b)	(c)
12.	47 × 3	207 × 5	789 × 4
13.	5 × 20	4 × 691	2 × 999
14.	36 ÷ 3	700 ÷ 4	450 ÷ 5
15.	78 ÷ 4	203 ÷ 2	128 ÷ 3

16. Ms. Owen bought 2 boxes of beads.
    Each box has an equal number of beads.
    There were 808 beads altogether.
    How many beads are there in each box?

17. There were 485 tablets in one carton.

   (a) Estimate the number of tablets in 4 such cartons.
   (b) Find the exact number of tablets in the 4 cartons.

18. Mary babysits for 4 hours a day.

   (a) How many hours does she babysit in 26 days?
   (b) If she is paid $3 an hour, how much money does she earn in 26 days?

19. David wants to buy 4 basketballs.
   He has only $55.
   How much more money does he need?

$18 each

20. A tailor bought 563 yd of cloth to make dresses.
   He used 3 yd to make each dress.

   (a) How many dresses did he make?
   (b) How many yards of cloth were left?
   (c) If he sold all the dresses at $5 each,
       how much money did he receive?

21. Kylie has $240.
   Nicole has 3 times as much money as Kylie.
   How much money do they have altogether?

22. 5 boys share 150 US stamps and 200 Canadian stamps equally.
   How many stamps does each boy get?

23. Steve packed 215 oranges into bags of 5 each.
   He sold all the oranges at $2 a bag.
   How much money did he receive?

24. What is the answer when a number is divided by itself?

25. What are all the possible remainders if a number is divided by 5?

26. A number is divided by 4. It has no remainder. Is that number an even number or an odd number? Explain your answer.

27. A farmer has 64 goats.
He has 4 times as many goats as cows.
Does he have more goats or more cows?
How many more?
Compare Kenji's and Sean's solutions. Whose solution is wrong?
Explain your answer.

Kenji's solution

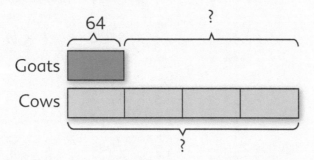

$64 \times 4 = 256$
He has more cows.
$256 - 64 = 192$
He has 192 more cows.

"4 times as many" means to multiply

Sean's solution

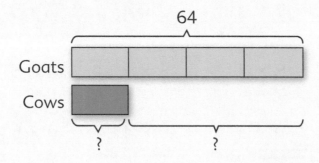

$64 \div 4 = 16$
He has more goats.
$64 - 16 = 48$
He has 48 more goats.

"4 times as many" does not always mean to multiply.

Review 3, pages 116—124

4 MULTIPLICATION TABLES OF 6, 7, 8, AND 9

1 Multiplying and Dividing by 6

1 × 1	1 × 2	1 × 3	1 × 4	1 × 5
2 × 1	2 × 2	2 × 3	2 × 4	2 × 5
3 × 1	3 × 2	3 × 3	3 × 4	3 × 5
4 × 1	4 × 2	4 × 3	4 × 4	4 × 5
5 × 1	5 × 2	5 × 3	5 × 4	5 × 5
6 × 1	6 × 2	6 × 3	6 × 4	6 × 5
7 × 1	7 × 2	7 × 3	7 × 4	7 × 5
8 × 1	8 × 2	8 × 3	8 × 4	8 × 5
9 × 1	9 × 2	9 × 3	9 × 4	9 × 5
10 × 1	10 × 2	10 × 3	10 × 4	10 × 5

1 × 6	1 × 7	1 × 8	1 × 9	1 × 10
2 × 6	2 × 7	2 × 8	2 × 9	2 × 10
3 × 6	3 × 7	3 × 8	3 × 9	3 × 10
4 × 6	4 × 7	4 × 8	4 × 9	4 × 10
5 × 6	5 × 7	5 × 8	5 × 9	5 × 10
6 × 6	6 × 7	6 × 8	6 × 9	6 × 10
7 × 6	7 × 7	7 × 8	7 × 9	7 × 10
8 × 6	8 × 7	8 × 8	8 × 9	8 × 10
9 × 6	9 × 7	9 × 8	9 × 9	9 × 10
10 × 6	10 × 7	10 × 8	10 × 9	10 × 10

Find the cards that have the answer 24.

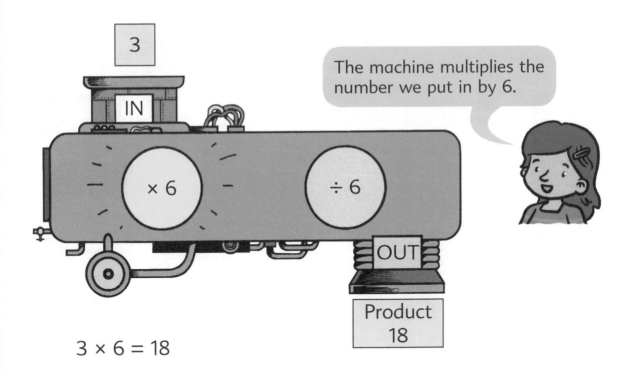

$3 \times 6 = 18$

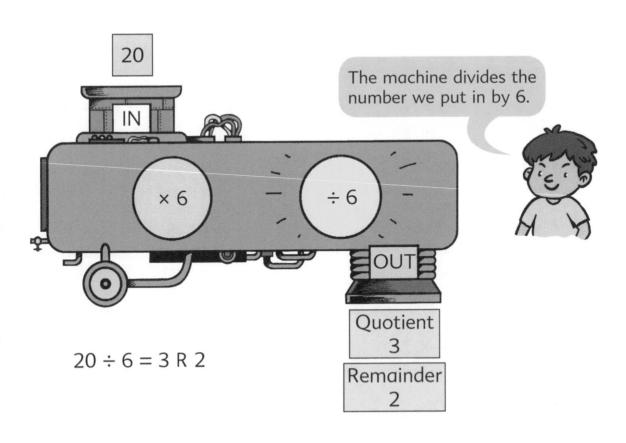

$20 \div 6 = 3 \text{ R } 2$

Multiply or divide.

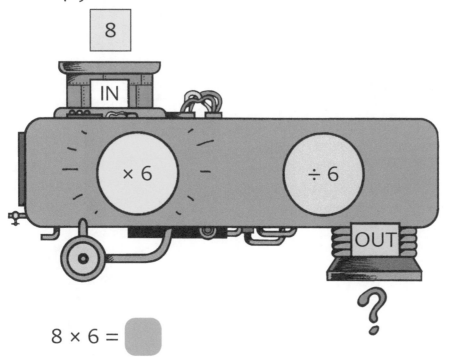

$8 \times 6 =$

$54 \div 6 =$

	0	1	2	3	4	5	6	7	8	9	10	
× 6	0	6	12	18	24	30					60	÷ 6

1. Fill in the missing numbers.

(a)

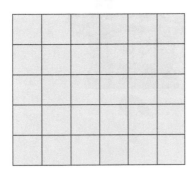

$4 \times 6 = $

(b)

$5 \times 6 = 6 \times 5$

$5 \times 6 = $

$6 \times 5 = $

2. Multiply.

(a)

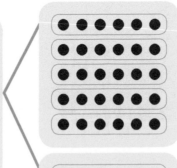

6×6

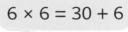

5×6

1×6

$6 \times 6 = 30 + 6$

$6 \times 6 = (5 \times 6) + (1 \times 6)$

$= $ $ + $

$= $

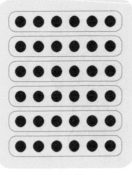

The total is 24.
The symbol has
to be + or ×.

126

(b)

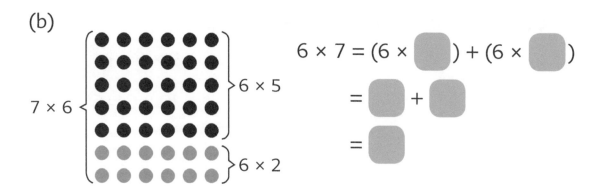

$6 \times 7 = (6 \times \boxed{}) + (6 \times \boxed{})$

$= \boxed{} + \boxed{}$

$= \boxed{}$

7 × 6

6 × 5

6 × 2

(c)

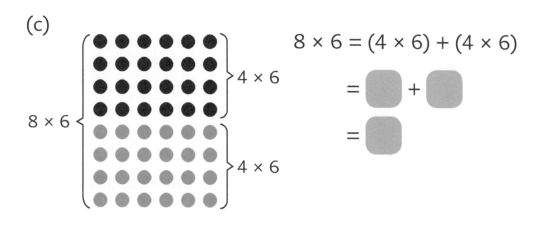

$8 \times 6 = (4 \times 6) + (4 \times 6)$

$= \boxed{} + \boxed{}$

$= \boxed{}$

8 × 6

4 × 6

4 × 6

(d)

$6 \times 9 = (10 \times 6) - (1 \times 6)$

$= \boxed{} - \boxed{}$

$= \boxed{}$

10 × 6

9 × 6

1 × 6

$6 \times 9 = 60 - 6$

3. Complete the multiplication equations.

$1 \times 6 = 6$ $5 \times 6 = 30$ $9 \times 6 = $

$2 \times 6 = 12$ $6 \times 6 = $ $10 \times 6 = 60$

$3 \times 6 = 18$ $7 \times 6 = $

$4 \times 6 = 24$ $8 \times 6 = $

$6 \times 1 = $ $6 \times 5 = $ $6 \times 9 = $

$6 \times 2 = $ $6 \times 6 = $ $6 \times 10 = $

$6 \times 3 = $ $6 \times 7 = $

$6 \times 4 = $ $6 \times 8 = $

Exercise 1, pages 125–126

4. Complete the equations.

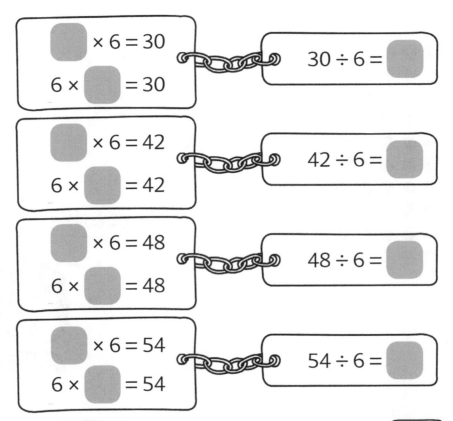

$\square \times 6 = 30$
$6 \times \square = 30$
$30 \div 6 = \square$

$\square \times 6 = 42$
$6 \times \square = 42$
$42 \div 6 = \square$

$\square \times 6 = 48$
$6 \times \square = 48$
$48 \div 6 = \square$

$\square \times 6 = 54$
$6 \times \square = 54$
$54 \div 6 = \square$

Exercise 2, pages 127–128

5. (a) Estimate the product of 285 and 6.

$300 \times 6 = \boxed{}$

285 is 300 when rounded to the nearest 100.

(b) Multiply 285 by 6.

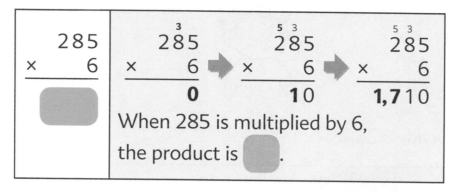

$$\begin{array}{r} 285 \\ \times \quad 6 \\ \hline \boxed{} \end{array}$$

When 285 is multiplied by 6, the product is $\boxed{}$.

Check the actual product with the estimate. Is it close?

6. Find the product of each of the following. Use estimation to see if your answer is reasonable.

(a) 34 and 6　　　　　　(b) 57 and 6
(c) 6 and 69　　　　　　(d) 108 and 6
(e) 472 and 6　　　　　(f) 6 and 910
(g) 987 and 6　　　　　(h) 6 and 732
(i) 6 and 593

Exercise 3, pages 129–131

7. (a) Estimate the quotient of 325 ÷ 6.

300 ÷ 6 = [ ]

325 ÷ 6 is about [ ].

6 × 5 = 30
6 × 6 = 36
I will use 300.

(b) Divide 325 by 6.

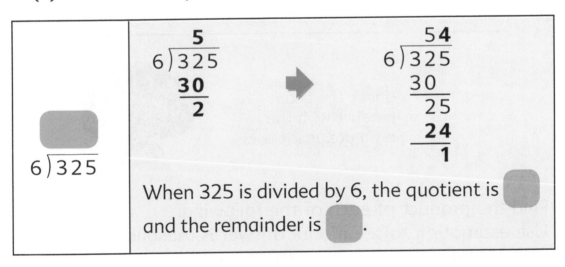

```
        5
    6)325
      30
       2
```

[ ]
6)325

```
        54
    6)325
      30
      25
      24
       1
```

When 325 is divided by 6, the quotient is [ ]
and the remainder is [ ].

8. Find the quotient and remainder for each of the following.
   Use estimation to see if your answer is reasonable.
   (a) 96 ÷ 6   (b) 89 ÷ 6
   (c) 75 ÷ 6   (d) 342 ÷ 6
   (e) 708 ÷ 6   (f) 615 ÷ 6
   (g) 700 ÷ 6   (h) 985 ÷ 6
   (i) 416 ÷ 6

Exercise 4, pages 132–134

9. Replace the letters with a number to make the equation true.
   (a) $6 \times k = 36$
   (b) $k \times 4 = 24$
   (c) $7 \times k = 42$
   (d) $k \times 6 = 60$

Solve the problems.

10. There are 6 players in one team.
    How many players are there in 14 teams?

11. 6 children share 84 balloons equally.
    How many balloons does each child get?

12. John earns $85 a week.
    How much money can he earn in 6 weeks?

13. Mr. Kim tied 192 books into bundles of 6 each.
    How many bundles were there?

14. Ms. Larson bought 6 m of cloth for $84.
    Find the cost of 5 m of cloth.

Exercise 5, pages 135–138

2 Multiplying and Dividing by 7

Sam made this table to help him collect money.

Number of cakes	1	2	3	4	5
Price	$7	$14	$21	$28	$35

(a) Amy bought 2 cakes.
     How much did she pay?

(b) Ms. Lee ordered 4 cakes for a party.
     How much did she pay?

(c) Sara paid Sam $35.
     How many cakes did Sam sell her?

(d) How many cakes could Ryan buy with $42?

1. Fill in the missing numbers.

(a)

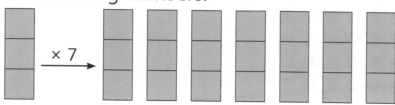

$3 \times 7 = $

(b)

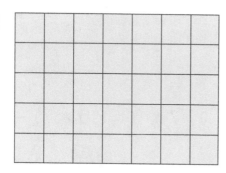

$5 \times 7 = $

$7 \times 5 = $

2. Fill in the missing numbers.

(a)

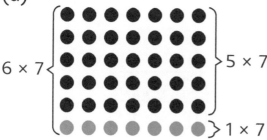

6×7 5×7 1×7

$6 \times 7 = (5 \times 7) + (1 \times 7)$

$= $ $+$

$= $

(b)

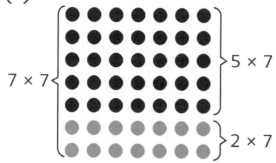

7×7 5×7 2×7

$7 \times 7 = (5 \times 7) + (2 \times 7)$

$= $ $+$

$= $

(c)

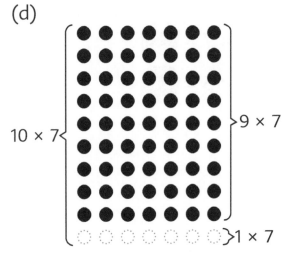

8×7
4×7
4×7

$8 \times 7 = (4 \times 7) + (4 \times 7)$

$= \boxed{} + \boxed{}$

$= \boxed{}$

(d)

10×7
9×7
1×7

$7 \times 9 = (10 \times 7) - (1 \times 7)$

$= \boxed{} - \boxed{}$

$= \boxed{}$

3. Fill in the missing numbers.

October						
Sun	Mon	Tue	Wed	Thu	Fri	Sat
1	2	3	4	5	6	7
8	9	10	11	12	13	14
15	16	17	18	19	20	21
22	23	24	25	26	27	28
29	30	31				

There are 7 days in a week.

There are days in 2 weeks.

There are  days in 4 weeks.

There are days in 10 weeks.

134

4. Complete the multiplication equations.

$1 \times 7 = 7$ $7 \times 1 = \boxed{}$

$2 \times 7 = 14$ $7 \times 2 = \boxed{}$

$3 \times 7 = 21$ $7 \times 3 = \boxed{}$

$4 \times 7 = \boxed{}$ $7 \times 4 = \boxed{}$

$5 \times 7 = \boxed{}$ $7 \times 5 = \boxed{}$

$6 \times 7 = \boxed{}$ $7 \times 6 = \boxed{}$

$7 \times 7 = \boxed{}$ $7 \times 7 = \boxed{}$

$8 \times 7 = \boxed{}$ $7 \times 8 = \boxed{}$

$9 \times 7 = \boxed{}$ $7 \times 9 = \boxed{}$

$10 \times 7 = \boxed{}$ $7 \times 10 = \boxed{}$

5. Complete the multiplication equations.

$\boxed{} \times 7 = 49$

$7 \times \boxed{} = 49$

$49 \div 7 = \boxed{}$

$\boxed{} \times 7 = 56$

$7 \times \boxed{} = 56$

$56 \div 7 = \boxed{}$

$\boxed{} \times 7 = 63$

$7 \times \boxed{} = 63$

$63 \div 7 = \boxed{}$

6. Find the value of
   (a) 6×7 (b) 7×7 (c) 7×9
   (d) $56 \div 7$ (e) $70 \div 7$ (f) $21 \div 7$

Exercise 6, pages 139–141

7. Find the product of 867 and 7.

```
      8 6 7         ⁴            ⁴ ⁴           ⁴ ⁴
    ×     7       8 6 7        8 6 7         8 6 7
   ┌───┐       ×     7      ×     7       ×     7
   │   │       ───────      ───────       ───────
   └───┘          9            6 9        6,0 6 9
```

When 867 is multiplied by 7,

the product is ⬚.

8. Multiply.
   (a) 56 × 7   (b) 63 × 7   (c) 7 × 71
   (d) 920 × 7   (e) 804 × 7   (f) 7 × 218

Exercise 7, pages 142–143

9. Divide 799 by 7.

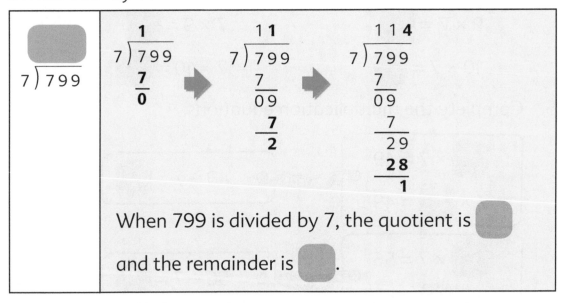

When 799 is divided by 7, the quotient is ⬚

and the remainder is ⬚.

10. Divide.
   (a) 75 ÷ 7   (b) 84 ÷ 7   (c) 64 ÷ 7
   (d) 91 ÷ 7   (e) 98 ÷ 7   (f) 80 ÷ 7

11. Divide.
   (a) 108 ÷ 7   (b) 231 ÷ 7   (c) 682 ÷ 7
   (d) 730 ÷ 7   (e) 954 ÷ 7   (f) 705 ÷ 7

Exercise 8, pages 144–145

12. Replace the letter *m* with a number to make the equation true.
    (a) $7 \times m = 56$ (b) $m \times 7 = 28$
    (c) $7 \times m = 42$ (d) $m \times 7 = 63$

Solve the problems.

13. A baker needs 7 eggs to bake a cake.
    He has 150 eggs.
    How many cakes can he bake?
    How many eggs will be left over?

14. There are 7 days in a week.
    How many days are there in 52 weeks?

15. Mr. Williams is 7 times as old as his grandson.
    He is 63 years old.
    How old is his grandson?

16. Chelsea bought 7 kg of shrimp.
    How much did she pay?

$26 for 1 kg

17. Lindsey spent $84 on 7 towels.
    What was the cost of 1 towel?

18. Taylor packed 112 lemons into bags of 7 each.
    She sold all the lemons at $3 a bag.
    How much money did she receive?

19. There were 7 boxes of blue pens and red pens.
    There were 12 pens in each box.
    If there were 36 red pens, how many blue pens were there?

Exercise 9, pages 146–149

③ Multiplying and Dividing by 8

$\times 2$ $\times 2$

$1 \times 2 = 2$	$1 \times 4 = 4$	$1 \times 8 = 8$
$2 \times 2 = 4$	$2 \times 4 = 8$	$2 \times 8 = 16$
$3 \times 2 = 6$	$3 \times 4 = 12$	$3 \times 8 = 24$
$4 \times 2 = 8$	$4 \times 4 = 16$	$4 \times 8 = 32$
$5 \times 2 = 10$	$5 \times 4 = 20$	$5 \times 8 = 40$
$6 \times 2 = 12$	$6 \times 4 = 24$	$6 \times 8 = 48$
$7 \times 2 = 14$	$7 \times 4 = 28$	$7 \times 8 = 56$
$8 \times 2 = 16$	$8 \times 4 = 32$	$8 \times 8 = ?$
$9 \times 2 = 18$	$9 \times 4 = 36$	$9 \times 8 = ?$
$10 \times 2 = 20$	$10 \times 4 = 40$	$10 \times 8 = 80$

Multiply by 8.

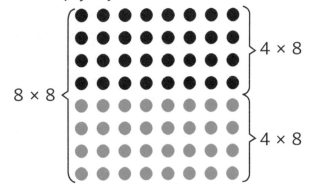

$8 \times 8 = (4 \times 8) + (4 \times 8)$

$= \square + \square$

$= \square$

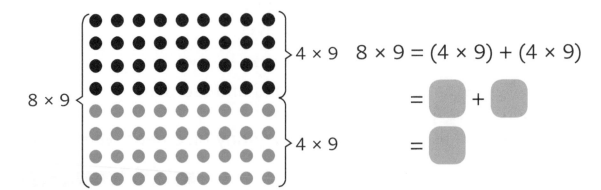

$8 \times 9 = (4 \times 9) + (4 \times 9)$

$= \square + \square$

$= \square$

1. Complete the table below.
   An octopus has 8 arms.

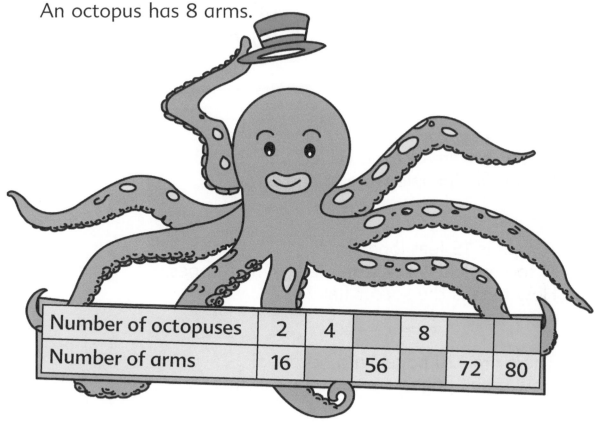

Number of octopuses	2	4		8		
Number of arms	16		56		72	80

2. Multiply.
   (a) 3 × 8   (b) 5 × 8   (c) 8 × 8
   (d) 8 × 4   (e) 8 × 7   (f) 8 × 9

3. Divide.
   (a) 80 ÷ 8   (b) 48 ÷ 8   (c) 24 ÷ 8
   (d) 72 ÷ 8   (e) 56 ÷ 8   (f) 40 ÷ 8

Exercise 10, pages 150—151

4. Multiply.
   (a) 56 × 8   (b) 79 × 8   (c) 8 × 68
   (d) 418 × 8   (e) 305 × 8   (f) 8 × 620

Exercise 11, pages 152—153

5. Divide.
   (a) 98 ÷ 8   (b) 112 ÷ 8   (c) 807 ÷ 8
   (d) 305 ÷ 8   (e) 664 ÷ 8   (f) 960 ÷ 8

Exercise 12, pages 154—155

6. Replace the letter m with a number to make the equation true.
   (a) $8 \times m = 32$ (b) $m \times 8 = 48$
   (c) $8 \times m = 64$ (d) $m \times 8 = 72$

Solve the problems.

7. There were 36 tables at a dinner party.
   8 people were at each table.
   How many people were at the party?

8. A rope is 15 feet long.
   A soccer field is the same length as 8 ropes.
   How long is the soccer field?

9. There are 120 pages in a notebook.
   How many pages are there in 8 such notebooks?

10. Kathy baked 390 cookies.
    She put them into boxes of 8 each.
    How many boxes did she have?
    How many cookies were left over?

11. A gardener bought 12 watering cans.
    If he gave the cashier $100, how much
    change did he receive?

$8

Exercise 13, pages 156–159

④ Multiplying and Dividing by 9

$1 \times 10 = 10$	$1 \times 9 = 9$	$10 - 1$
$2 \times 10 = 20$	$2 \times 9 = 18$	$20 - 2$
$3 \times 10 = 30$	$3 \times 9 = 27$	$30 - 3$
$4 \times 10 = 40$	$4 \times 9 = 36$	$40 - 4$
$5 \times 10 = 50$	$5 \times 9 = 45$	$50 - 5$
$6 \times 10 = 60$	$6 \times 9 = 54$	$60 - 6$
$7 \times 10 = 70$	$7 \times 9 = 63$	$70 - 7$
$8 \times 10 = 80$	$8 \times 9 = ?$	$80 - 8$
$9 \times 10 = 90$	$9 \times 9 = ?$	$90 - 9$
$10 \times 10 = 100$	$10 \times 9 = 90$	$100 - 10$

Multiply by 9.

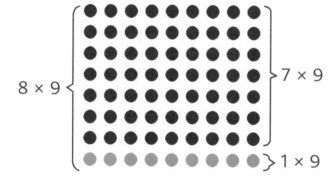

$8 \times 9 = (7 \times 9) + (1 \times 9)$

= ☐ + ☐

= ☐

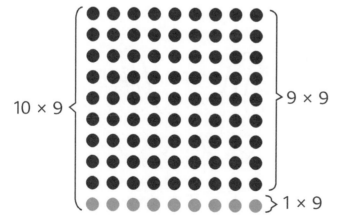

$9 \times 9 = (10 \times 9) - (1 \times 9)$

= ☐ - ☐

= ☐

141

1. Add the tens digit and ones digit of each product.

   The answer is .

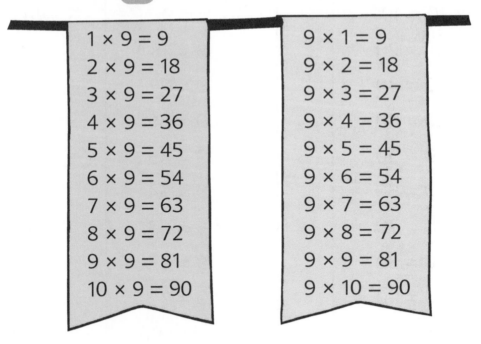

1 × 9 = 9	9 × 1 = 9
2 × 9 = 18	9 × 2 = 18
3 × 9 = 27	9 × 3 = 27
4 × 9 = 36	9 × 4 = 36
5 × 9 = 45	9 × 5 = 45
6 × 9 = 54	9 × 6 = 54
7 × 9 = 63	9 × 7 = 63
8 × 9 = 72	9 × 8 = 72
9 × 9 = 81	9 × 9 = 81
10 × 9 = 90	9 × 10 = 90

2. Here is an interesting way to multiply by 9.

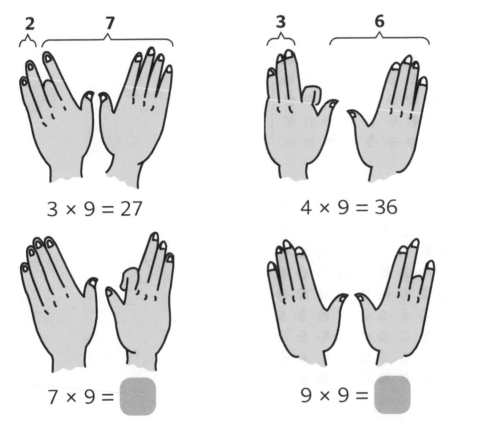

3 × 9 = 27   4 × 9 = 36

7 × 9 =   9 × 9 =

3. Fill in the missing numbers.

(a)

●●●●●●●●●●
●●●●●●●●●● } 18   9 × 2 = 18

●●●●●●●●●●
●●●●●●●●●● } 18   9 × 4 = 18 × ⬜

●●●●●●●●●●
●●●●●●●●●● } 18   9 × 6 = 18 × ⬜

●●●●●●●●●●
●●●●●●●●●● } 18   9 × 8 = 18 × ⬜

●●●●●●●●●●
●●●●●●●●●● } 18   9 × 10 = 18 × ⬜

(b)

●●●●●●●●●●
●●●●●●●●●● } 27   9 × 3 = 27
●●●●●●●●●●

●●●●●●●●●●
●●●●●●●●●● } 27   9 × 6 = 27 × ⬜
●●●●●●●●●●

4. Multiply.
   (a) 2 × 9   (b) 4 × 9   (c) 9 × 3
   (d) 8 × 9   (e) 9 × 9   (f) 9 × 7

5. Divide.
   (a) 90 ÷ 9   (b) 63 ÷ 9   (c) 45 ÷ 9
   (d) 54 ÷ 9   (e) 72 ÷ 9   (f) 81 ÷ 9

6. Multiply.   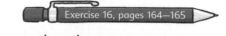 Exercise 14, pages 160–161
   (a) 54 × 9   (b) 73 × 9   (c) 9 × 80
   (d) 201 × 9   (e) 678 × 9   (f) 9 × 609

7. Divide.   Exercise 15, pages 162–163
   (a) 97 ÷ 9   (b) 108 ÷ 9   (c) 89 ÷ 9
   (d) 620 ÷ 9   (e) 903 ÷ 9   (f) 145 ÷ 9

                                         Exercise 16, pages 164–165

8. Replace the letter m with a number to make the equation true.
   (a) 9 × m = 81   (b) m × 9 = 54
   (c) 9 × m = 63   (d) m × 9 = 45

Solve the problems.

9. Mary bought 9 pieces of string, each 18 m long.
   How many meters of string did she buy?

10. 25 boys went camping.
    Each boy brought 9 cans of food.
    How many cans did they bring altogether?

11. Tyrone bought 9 T-shirts for $144.
    How much did 1 T-shirt cost?

12. David cut a wire 918 m long into pieces.
    Each piece was 9 m long.
    How many pieces did he get?

13. Cameron uses 185 gallons of gas a month.
    How much gas does he use in 9 months?

14. A tailor bought 9 packets of buttons.
    There were 80 buttons in each packet.
    He used 8 buttons on a dress.
    How many dresses did he make if he used all the buttons?

15. The product of a number and 9 is even.
    Is that number odd or even?

16. Dorothy bought a refrigerator.
    She paid $245 in the first month and $103 each month for
    another 9 months.
    What was the cost of the refrigerator?

Exercise 17, pages 166—169

REVIEW 4

1. How many legs do 9 spiders have if each spider has 8 legs?
   (A) 63   (B) 72   (C) 81   (D) 90

2. What is the product of 8 hundreds and 7?
   (A) 56   (B) 560   (C) 807   (D) 5,600

3. Divide 733 by 9. What is the quotient?
   (A) 4   (B) 81   (C) 724   (D) 810

4. I am a number that can be divided by 3, 8 and 7. What number am I?
   (A) 56   (B) 84   (C) 112   (D) 168

5. $n \times 8 = \bigstar$
   $\bigstar \times 6 = 432$
   What does n stand for?
   (A) 9   (B) 48   (C) 72   (D) 324

6. Select True or False.
   (a) $40 \div 8 > 20 \div 4$ True / False
   (b) $7 \times 7 = 4 + 9$ True / False
   (c) $0 \times 9 < 2 + 0$ True / False

7. Select True or False.
   (a) $32 \div 8 = 2 \times 2$ True / False
   (b) $45 - 9 > 6 \times 6$ True / False
   (c) $4 + 4 = 56 \div 7$ True / False

8. Which sign goes in the ⬤, **+**, **−**, **×**, or **÷**?

   (a) 42 ⬤ 6 = 7   (b) 6 ⬤ 30 = 6 × 6

   (c) 50 ⬤ 2 = 6 × 8   (d) 9 ⬤ 8 = 8 × 9

   (e) 48 ⬤ 8 = 8 ⬤ 7   (f) 72 ⬤ 9 = 9 ⬤ 7

9. What number goes in the ▢?

   (a) 54 ÷ ▢ = 3 × 2   (b) 72 = 6 × 8 + ▢ × 8

   (c) 7 × 8 = 42 + ▢   (d) 9 × 6 = ▢ × 18

10. Find the product of each of the following.
    Use estimation to see if your answer is reasonable.
    (a) 278 × 7   (b) 1,173 × 8   (c) 678 × 9

11. Use mental calculation to find the value of each of the
    following.
    (a) 400 × 8   (b) 60 × 7   (c) 200 × 6
    (d) 490 ÷ 7   (e) 300 ÷ 6   (f) 720 ÷ 9

Find the value of

	(a)	(b)	(c)
12.	67 × 7	57 × 8	82 × 9
13.	513 × 6	657 × 9	901 × 7
14.	64 ÷ 8	58 ÷ 7	42 ÷ 6
15.	483 ÷ 7	304 ÷ 6	899 ÷ 9

16. Matthew worked for 8 days.
    He was paid $36 each day.
    How much money did he receive?

17. A grocer had 145 oranges.
    He packed the oranges into bags of 6 oranges each.
    How many bags were there?
    How many oranges were left over?

18. A tree farm has 126 evergreen trees.
    They are planted in rows of 9 trees.
    How many rows of trees are there?

19. There are 136 roses.
    There are 9 times as many sunflowers as roses.
    How many sunflowers are there?

20. Ms. Sanchez wants to buy umbrellas.
    Each umbrella costs $7.
    How many umbrellas can she buy with $168?

    $7 each

21. Tony wants to buy 6 chairs that cost $28 each.
    He has only $100.
    How much more money does he need?

22. Melissa bought 27 apples at 3 for $2.
    How much did she pay in all?

23. Ms. Barret bought 8 boxes of cookies for a party.
    There were 12 cookies in each box.
    After the party, there were 28 cookies left.
    How many cookies were eaten at the party?

24. A jacket costs 7 times as much as a T-shirt.
    If the T-shirt costs $26, what is the total cost of the T-shirt and
    the jacket?

25. 4 people bought a birthday present for their friend.
    They paid the cashier $100 and received $48 change.
    If they shared the cost equally, how much did each person pay?

26. 8 people went to the seaside.
    They rented a boat for 6 hours.
    If they shared the cost equally,
    how much did each person spend?

BOATS
for hire
$12 for 1 hour

27. $9 \times 9 = (10 \times 9) - (1 \times 9)$ because
    9 groups of 9 = 10 groups of 9 — 1 group of 9.

    Use mental calculation to find the missing number in the
    following:

    $8 \times 9 = (10 \times 9) - (\boxed{} \times 9)$

    $7 \times 9 = (10 \times 9) - (\boxed{} \times 9)$

    $6 \times 9 = (10 \times 9) - (\boxed{} \times 9)$

    What is the missing number in $\boxed{}$?

    $80 \times 9 = (100 \times 8) - (\boxed{} \times 8)$

    Explain how you got the answer.

Review 4, pages 170–175

5 LENGTH

1 Meters and Centimeters

Estimate the length of the board in the classroom.
Then check by measuring it with a meterstick.

Is the length closer to 2 m or 3 m?

Estimate the height of the door in your classroom.
Check by measuring it with a meterstick.

The **meter (m)** and **centimeter (cm)** are units of length.

1 m = 100 cm

1. Which of these tools would you use to measure the following?
   (a) the width of a room
   (b) the size of your waist
   (c) the length and width of your math book
   (d) the width of a door

2. Would you use meters or centimeters to measure the following?
   (a) the length of a playground
   (b) the length of a crayon
   (c) the length of a butterfly
   (d) the length of the hallway

> You can measure in meters and centimeters!

3. Joe's height is 1 m 25 cm.

   (a) 1 m 25 cm is ⬜ cm more than 1 m.

   (b) 1 m 25 cm = ⬜ cm

4. (a) Write 2 m in centimeters.

   2 m = ⬜ cm

   (b) Write 300 cm in meters.

   300 cm = ⬜ m

5. (a) Estimate the length of your classroom.
   Then measure the length in meters and centimeters.
   Write the distance in meters and centimeters.

   (b) Estimate how far you can walk in 5 steps.
   Then walk 5 steps and measure the distance in meters and centimeters.
   Write the distance in meters and centimeters.

6. David's long jump result is 1 m 45 cm.
Write the distance in centimeters.

1 m 45 cm = ⬜ cm

7. Write in centimeters.
   (a) 1 m 90 cm   (b) 1 m 55 cm   (c) 2 m 86 cm
   (d) 2 m 89 cm   (e) 3 m 8 cm   (f) 4 m 6 cm

8. A car is 395 cm long.
Write the length in meters and centimeters.

300 cm = 3 m

395 cm = ⬜ m ⬜ cm

9. Write in meters and centimeters.
   (a) 180 cm   (b) 195 cm   (c) 262 cm
   (d) 299 cm   (e) 304 cm   (f) 409 cm

10. Which sign goes in each ⬤, >, <, or =?

    (a) 178 cm ⬤ 1 m 78 cm   (b) 350 cm ⬤ 3 m 5 cm

11. The table shows the results of the long jump finals.

Name	Distance
Ryan	1 m 89 cm
Andy	2 m 8 cm
Tyrone	1 m 96 cm

Arrange the distances in order. Begin with the shortest.

Exercise 1, page 176

12. Find the value of 1 m − 35 cm.

100 cm − 35 cm = [ ]

35 cm + [ ] = 100 cm

1 m = 100 cm

100 = 90 + 10

$$\begin{array}{r} 9 \text{ tens } 10 \text{ ones} \\ - \quad 3 \text{ tens } 5 \text{ ones} \\ \hline 6 \text{ tens } 5 \text{ ones} \end{array}$$

$35 \xrightarrow{+5} 40 \xrightarrow{+60} 100$

or

$35 \xrightarrow{+60} 95 \xrightarrow{+5} 100$

1 m − 35 cm = [ ] cm

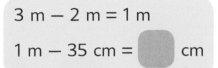

3 m − 2 m = 1 m

1 m − 35 cm = [ ] cm

13. Find the value of 3 m − 2 m 35 cm.

3 m − 2 m 35 cm = [ ] cm

14. Find the missing numbers.

(a) 1 m − 40 cm = [ ] cm

(b) 1 m − 85 cm = [ ] cm

(c) 1 m − 43 cm = [ ] cm

(d) 1 m − 67 cm = [ ] cm

(e) 32 cm + [ ] cm = 1 m

(f) 91 cm + [ ] cm = 1 m

(g) 2 m − 1 m 25 cm = [ ] cm

(h) 3 m − 2 m 46 cm = [ ] cm

(i) 6 m − 5 m 4 cm = [ ] cm

(j) 9 m 73 cm + [ ] cm = 10 m

Exercise 2, page 177

152

15. Lily has a red ribbon 3 m 40 cm long and a yellow ribbon 1 m 85 cm long.

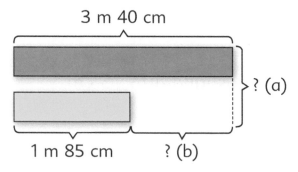

3 m 40 cm

? (a)

1 m 85 cm   ? (b)

(a) Find the total length of the ribbons.

3 m 40 cm + 1 m 85 cm

$$3 \text{ m } 40 \text{ cm} \xrightarrow{+1 \text{ m}} 4 \text{ m } 40 \text{ cm} \xrightarrow{+85 \text{ cm}} 5 \text{ m } 25 \text{ cm}$$

The total length of the ribbons is

 m ⬜ cm.

(b) How much longer is the red ribbon than the yellow ribbon?

3 m 40 cm − 1 m 85 cm

$$3 \text{ m } 40 \text{ cm} \xrightarrow{-1 \text{ m}} 2 \text{ m } 40 \text{ cm} \xrightarrow{-85 \text{ cm}} 1 \text{ m } 55 \text{ cm}$$

The red ribbon is ⬜ m ⬜ cm longer than the yellow ribbon.

16. Add or subtract in compound units.
   (a) 4 m 32 cm + 5 m
   (b) 3 m 65 cm + 14 cm
   (c) 7 m 85 cm + 45 cm
   (d) 2 m 18 cm + 4 m 28 cm
   (e) 1 m 65 cm + 1 m 55 cm
   (f) 6 m 28 cm + 2 m 73 cm
   (g) 9 m 15 cm − 3 m
   (h) 5 m 39 cm − 15 cm
   (i) 5 m − 45 cm
   (j) 6 m 15 cm − 2 m 20 cm
   (k) 4 m 35 cm − 80 cm
   (l) 8 m 5 cm − 5 m 75 cm

17. Jon is 18 cm taller than Ai Mei. Ai Mei's height is 1 m 63 cm.
    What is Jon's height in centimeters?

    Jon is  cm tall.

18. Natalie had a piece of ribbon measuring 4 m 75 cm.
    She used 2 m 90 cm.
    How long was the ribbon that was left?

    ☐ m ☐ cm of ribbon was left.

19. Mr. Rogers used 650 cm of cloth to make curtains.
    He had 375 cm of cloth left.
    How much cloth did he have at first? Leave your answers in
    meters and centimeters.

    He had ☐ m ☐ cm of cloth at first.

20. Benjamin is 190 cm tall.
    He is twice as tall as his daughter.
    How tall is his daughter?

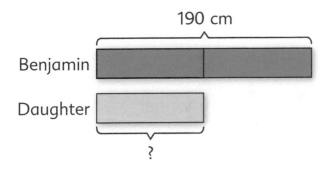

    2 units = ☐ cm

    1 unit = ☐ cm ÷ 2

         = ☐ cm

    His daughter is ☐ cm tall.

21. Mrs. Grant has 350 cm of cloth.
    She cuts it into 7 pieces.
    How long is each piece of cloth?

350 = 35 tens

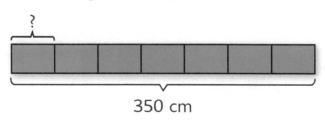

?

350 cm

7 units = ☐ cm

1 unit = ☐ cm ÷ 7

= ☐ cm

Each piece is ☐ cm long.

22. The total length of 8 shoelaces of equal length is 720 cm.
    How long is one shoelace?

    One shoelace is ☐ cm long.

23. Mrs. Kim walks her dog in the park for 850 m a day.
    How far does she walk her dog in a week?

    She walks her dog ☐ m in a week.

Exercise 3, pages 178—180

2 Kilometers

The **kilometer (km)**, meter (m), and centimeter (cm) are units of length.

1 km = 1,000 m
1 m = 100 cm

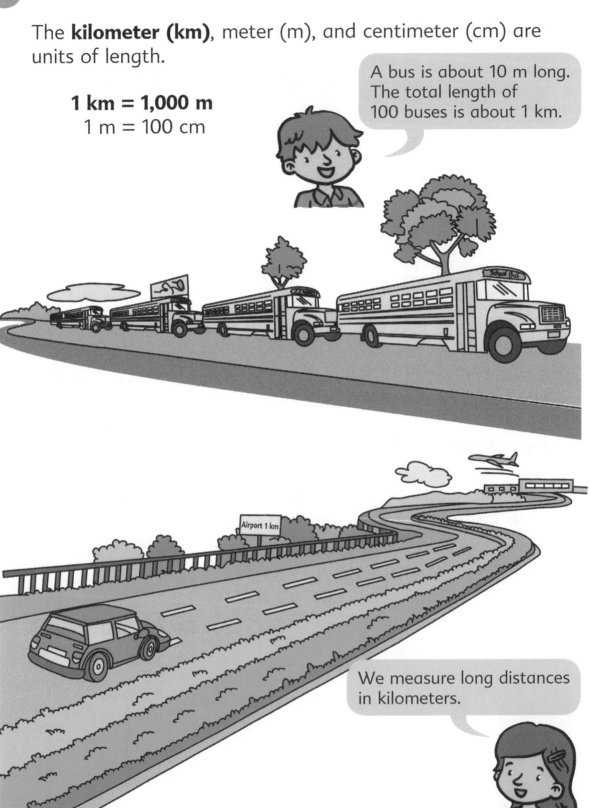

A bus is about 10 m long. The total length of 100 buses is about 1 km.

Airport 1 km

We measure long distances in kilometers.

1. Fill in the blanks.

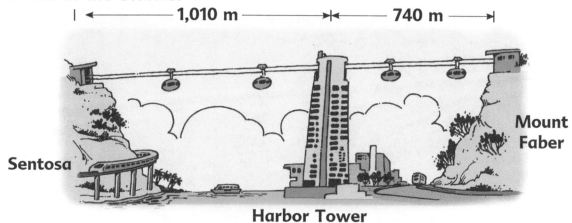

1,010 m — **740 m**

Sentosa

Harbor Tower

Mount Faber

(a) The distance between Sentosa and Harbor Tower
is ☐ km ☐ m.

(b) The distance between Mount Faber and Sentosa
is ☐ km ☐ m.

2. Fill in the blanks.

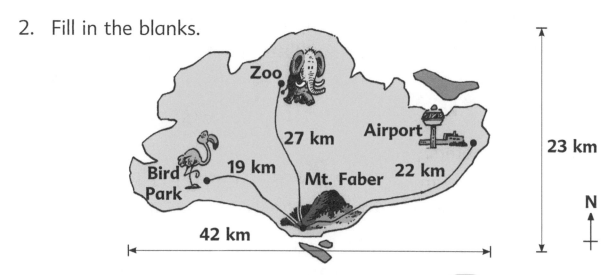

Zoo

Airport

27 km

23 km

Bird Park   19 km   Mt. Faber   22 km

N

42 km

(a) The distance across Singapore is about ☐ km
from west to east.

It is about ☐ km from north to south.

(b) The distance from the Bird Park to the airport
is about ☐ km.

3.

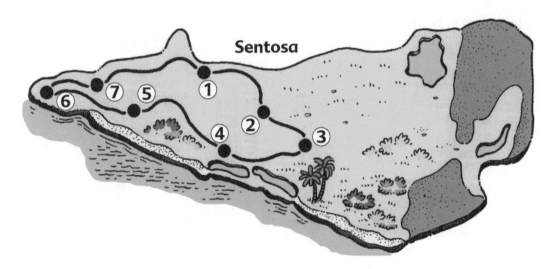

Sentosa

The total length of the train route on Sentosa Island is about
6 km 100 m.

6 km = 6,000 m

Write the length in meters.

4. The distance around a running track is 400 m.
Ryan ran round the track 3 times.

He ran ⬜ km ⬜ m.

5. Write in meters.
   (a) 1 km 600 m   (b) 2 km 550 m   (c) 2 km 605 m
   (d) 3 km 85 m   (e) 3 km 20 m   (f) 4 km 5 m

6. Write in kilometers and meters.
   (a) 1,830 m   (b) 2,304 m   (c) 2,780 m
   (d) 3,096 m   (e) 3,040 m   (f) 4,009 m

7. Which sign goes in each ⬤, >, <, or =?

   (a) 2,630 m ⬤ 2 km 63 m

   (b) 4,040 m ⬤ 4 km 400 m

Exercise 4, pages 181–184

8. Find the value of 1 km − 350 m.

1,000 m − 350 m = ⬜

350 m + ⬜ = 1,000 m

1 km − 350 m = ⬜ m

1 km = 1,000 m

1,000 = 900 + 90 + 10

	9 hundreds	10 tens
−	3 hundreds	5 tens
	6 hundreds	5 tens

9. Find the value of 1 km − 5 m.

1 km − 5 m = ⬜ m

1,000

900 90 10

10 − 5 = 5

10. Find the value of 1 km − 355 m.

1 km − 355 m = ⬜ m

1,000

900 90 10

900 − 300 = 600
90 − 50 = 40
10 − 5 = 5

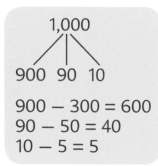

11. Find the value of 2 km − 1 km 625 m.

2 km − 1 km 625 m = ⬜ m

2 km − 1 km = 1 km

1 km − 625 m = ⬜ m

12. Find the value of 1 km 24 m − 789 m.

$$\begin{array}{r} 1,024 \\ -789 \\ \hline \end{array}$$

1 km 24 m − 789 m = ⬚ m

13. Find the sum of 1 km 456 m and 879 m.

$$\begin{array}{r} 1,456 \\ +879 \\ \hline \end{array}$$

1 km 456 m + 879 m = ⬚ km ⬚ m

14. Find the missing numbers.

(a) 1 km − 240 m = ⬚ m   (b) 1 km − 248 m = ⬚ m

(c) 1 km − 45 m = ⬚ m   (d) 1 km − 7 m = ⬚ m

(e) 324 m + ⬚ m = 1 km   (f) 901 m + ⬚ m = 1 km

(g) 2 km − 1 km 125 m = ⬚ m

(h) 3 km − 2 km 45 m = ⬚ m

(i) 1 km 485 m + 458 m = ⬚ km ⬚ m

(j) 4 km 903 m + 99 m = ⬚ km ⬚ m

Exercise 5, pages 185–186

15.

Bank   **Post Office**   **Library**

Find the distance between the bank and the library.

2 km 450 m + 1 km 850 m = ⬜ km ⬜ m

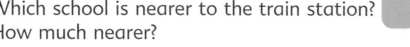

2 km 450 m $\xrightarrow{+1\,km}$ 3 km 450 m $\xrightarrow{+850\,m}$ 4 km 300 m

The distance between the bank and the library

is ⬜ km ⬜ m.

16.

School A   **Train Station**   **School B**

Which school is nearer to the train station? ⬜
How much nearer?

1 km 40 m − 920 m = ⬜ m

⬜ is ⬜ m nearer to the train station.

17. Add or subtract in compound units.

(a) 4 km 325 m + 5 km   (b) 3 km 650 m + 240 m
(c) 7 km 800 m + 300 m   (d) 2 km 180 m + 4 km 65 m
(e) 9 km 150 m − 3 km   (f) 5 km 950 m − 150 m
(g) 5 km − 400 m   (h) 6 km 150 m − 2 km 200 m
(i) 4 km 350 m − 800 m   (j) 8 km 5 m − 5 km 750 m

18. Maurice's house is 18 km from a library.
The park is nearer to his house than the library by 3 km 50 m.
Find the distance between the park and Maurice's house.
The distance between the park and Maurice's house is

☐ km ☐ m.

19. Alice cycled 1 km 250 m from her house to the video rental store.
She cycled another 3 km 900 km to the supermarket.
Find the total distance Alice cycled.

Alice cycled ☐ km ☐ m.

20. Ian ran 21 km 50 m.
Kim ran 3 km 600 m less than Ian.
How far did Kim run?

Kim ran ☐ km ☐ m.

21. Mark ran 21 km each week for 5 weeks.
What is the total distance Mark ran?

21 km

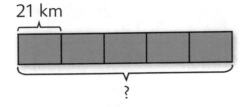

?

21 km + 21 km + 21 km + 21 km

+ 21 km = ☐ km

1 unit = ☐ km

5 units = ☐ km × 5 = ☐ km

He ran a total distance of ☐ km.

22. The distance between Wendy's house and the library
is 6 km.
The distance between her house and the international airport
is twice as far. Find the distance between her house and the
international airport.

The distance is ☐ km.

Exercise 6, pages 187–189

3 Other Units of Length

Get a yardstick and find out how long 1 yard is.
Estimate the length of the teacher's desk in your classroom.
Check by measuring it with a yardstick.

Is the length of your teacher's desk more than 2 yards?

Get a ruler and find out how long 1 foot is.
Estimate the length of your math book.
Check by measuring with your ruler.

Is your math book less than a foot long?

Take a look at your ruler again.
Is your math book about 10 inches long?

The **yard (yd)**, **foot (ft)**, and **inch (in.)** are units of length.

1 yd = 3 ft
1 ft = 12 in.

Compare a yard with a meter.
Which is shorter?

Compare an inch with a centimeter.
Which is longer?

1. A table is 1 yd 2 ft long.

   (a) 1 yd 2 ft is ☐ ft more than 1 yd.

   (b) 1 yd 2 ft = ☐ ft

2. Write 8 yd in feet.

   8 yd = ☐ ft

   To change yards to feet, we multiply by 3.

   1 yd = 1 × 3 = 3 ft
   2 yd = 2 × 3 = 6 ft

3. A ribbon is 11 yd 2 ft. Write the length in feet.

   11 yd 2 ft = ☐ ft.

4. (a) Write 7 ft in inches.

   7 ft = ☐ in.

   (b) Write 7 ft 3 in. in inches.

   7 ft 3 in. = ☐ in.

   To change feet to inches, we multiply by 12.

   1 ft = 1 × 12 = 12 in.
   2 ft = 2 × 12 = 24 in.

5. Find the missing numbers.

   (a) 6 yd = ☐ ft

   (b) 32 yd = ☐ ft

   (c) 9 yd 2 ft = ☐ ft

   (d) 12 yd 1 ft = ☐ ft

   (e) 1 ft 5 in. = ☐ in.

   (f) 4 ft = ☐ in.

   (g) 4 ft 9 in. = ☐ in.

   (h) 6 ft 4 in. = ☐ in.

6. Which sign goes in each ◯, >, <, or =?

   (a) 26 in. ◯ 2 ft 6 in.

   (b) 4 yd 2 ft ◯ 14 ft

Exercise 7, page 190

7. How long are two paper strips, each
   11 inches long, taped together?

   11 in. + 11 in. = ☐ ft ☐ in.

   11 in. + 1 in. = 1 ft
   11 in. + 11 in.
       ╱   ╲
     1 in.   10 in.

8. Find the value of 1 ft − 8 in.

   1 ft − 8 in. = ☐ in.

   1 ft = 12 in.

   8 in. + ☐ = 1 ft

9. (a) 6 ft − 8 in. = ☐ ft ☐ in.

   (b) 6 ft 4 in. − 8 in. = ☐ ft ☐ in.

   6 ft − 8 in.
      ╱   ╲
    5 ft   1 ft

10. A blue ribbon is 4 ft 7 in. long and a red ribbon
    is 1 ft 10 in. long.

    (a) Find the total length of the ribbons.

   4 ft 7 in. + 1 ft 10 in. = ☐ ft ☐ in.

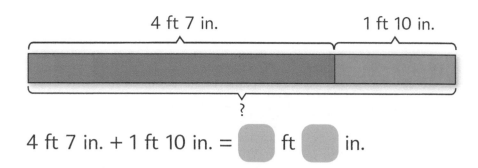

   4 ft 7 in. $\xrightarrow{+1\,ft}$ 5 ft 7 in. $\xrightarrow{+10\,in.}$ 6 ft 5 in.

   The total length of the ribbons is ☐ ft ☐ in.

165

(b) How much longer is the blue ribbon than the red ribbon?

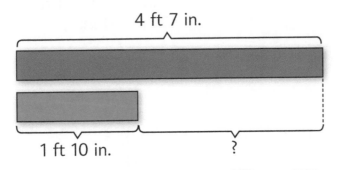

4 ft 7 in.

1 ft 10 in.   ?

4 ft 7 in. − 1 ft 10 in. = ⬚ ft ⬚ in.

4 ft 7 in. $\xrightarrow{-1\,ft}$ 3 ft 7 in. $\xrightarrow{-10\,in.}$ 2 ft 9 in.

The blue ribbon is ⬚ ft ⬚ in. longer than the red ribbon.

11. Find the missing numbers.

(a) 7 in. + ⬚ in. = 12 in.

(b) 3 in. + ⬚ in. = 12 in.

(c) 4 ft 6 in. + ⬚ in. = 5 ft

(d) 4 ft 6 in. + 8 in. = ⬚ ft ⬚ in.

(e) 1 ft 7 in. − 10 in. = ⬚ in.

(f) 5 ft 7 in. − 3 ft 10 in. = ⬚ ft ⬚ in.

Exercise 8, pages 191–192

12. 1 mile = 5,280 feet

What is the distance between Sandy and the Airport?

120 ⬤ 68 = ▢

13. Fill in the blank.

San Francisco   Denver   New York

←———— 1,260 mi ————→

←————————— 2,930 mi —————————→

The distance between San Francisco and New York

is ▢ mi.

Find the distance between New York and Denver.

14. Mary is 4 ft 5 in. tall. Pam is 3 ft 10 in. tall.
    How much taller is Mary than Pam?

    Mary is ☐ in. taller than Pam.

15. Anna made a "Welcome Home" banner for her brother.
    She taped together four pieces of paper 1 ft 5 in. long each.
    What was the final length of her banner?

    The final length of her banner was ☐ ft ☐ in.

16. An airplane flew from New York to Dallas, then from
    Dallas to San Francisco, and then directly back to New York.

    The distance from New York to Dallas is 1,370 mi.

    The distance from Dallas to San Francisco is 1,483 mi.

    The distance from New York to San Francisco is 2,569 mi.

    How much farther did the airplane fly to get from New York
    to San Francisco via Dallas than to go directly from San
    Francisco back to New York?

    The airplane flew ☐ mi farther.

Exercise 9, page 193

REVIEW 5

1. Which of the following is the shortest length?
   (A) 8 km   (B) 80 m   (C) 800 cm   (D) 8,000 m

2. The classroom door is about _____ wide.
   (A) 32 in.   (B) 32 ft   (C) 32 yd   (D) 32 mi

3. Express 4 m 70 cm in centimeters.
   (A) 407 cm   (B) 470 cm
   (C) 4,070 cm   (D) 4,700 cm

4. The distance between a school and a grocery store is 2,005 m. The school is _____ far from the store.
   (A) 2 km 5 m   (B) 2 km 50 m
   (C) 20 km 5 m   (D) 20 km 50 m

5. Clive is 5 ft 9 in. tall. Ronald is 4 in. taller. How tall is Ronald?
   (A) 5 ft 5 in.   (B) 6 ft 1 in.
   (C) 6 ft 3 in.   (D) 9 ft 9 in.

6. Select True or False.
   (a) 600 cm = 6 m   True / False
   (b) 7 km < 7,000 m   True / False

7. Select True or False.
   (a) 3 ft > 38 in.   True / False
   (b) 5 yd = 15 ft   True / False

8. Write in centimeters.
   (a) 4 m   (b) 1 m 40 cm   (c) 2 m 25 cm

9. Write in meters.
   (a) 3 km   (b) 1 km 450 m   (c) 2 km 506 m

10. Write in meters and centimeters.
    (a) 120 cm   (b) 225 cm   (c) 309 cm

11. Write in kilometers and meters.

   (a) 1,680 m   (b) 1,085 m   (c) 2,204 m

12. Write in feet.

   (a) 5 yd   (b) 87 yd 2 ft   (c) 308 yd 1 ft

13. Write in inches.

   (a) 9 ft   (b) 6 ft 10 in.   (c) 9 ft 9 in.

14. Fill in the missing numbers.

   (a) 3 m 95 cm = ☐ cm   (b) 4 m 5 cm = ☐ cm

   (c) 2 km 60 m = ☐ m   (d) 3 km 78 m = ☐ m

   (e) 618 cm = ☐ m ☐ cm   (f) 936 cm = ☐ m ☐ cm

   (g) 3,090 m = ☐ km ☐ m   (h) 3,999 m = ☐ km ☐ m

   (i) 4 yd = ☐ ft   (j) 48 yd 6 ft = ☐ ft

   (k) 6 ft = ☐ in.   (l) 3 ft 7 in. = ☐ in.

15. Find the missing numbers.

   (a) 1 ft − 7 in. = ☐ in.   (b) 13 ft − 12 ft 8 in. = ☐ in.

16. Find the missing numbers.

   (a) 1 m − 65 cm = ☐ cm

   (b) 2 m − 1 m 75 cm = ☐ cm

   (c) 3 m − 2 m 92 cm = ☐ cm

   (d) 1 km − 800 m = ☐ cm

   (e) 2 km − 1 km 45 m = ☐ cm

   (f) 5 km − 4 km 940 m = ☐ cm

17. Add or subtract in compound units.
    (a) 1 m − 55 cm
    (b) 2 m − 95 cm
    (c) 1 km − 600 m
    (d) 12 km − 275 m
    (e) 2 m 75 cm + 3 m
    (f) 3 m 4 cm + 65 cm
    (g) 5 m 85 cm − 5 cm
    (h) 5 m 90 cm − 76 cm
    (i) 1 m 26 cm + 2 m 65 cm
    (j) 2 km 650 m + 3 km
    (k) 3 km 300 m + 800 m
    (l) 5 km 950 m − 4 km
    (m) 6 km 25 m − 3 km 350 m
    (n) 5 km 40 m − 3 km 990 m

18. Add or subtract in compound units.
    (a) 5 ft 11 in. + 7 ft
    (b) 9 ft 5 in. + 6 in.
    (c) 8 ft 7 in. + 3 ft 8 in.
    (d) 11 ft 11 in. − 6 in.
    (e) 10 ft 4 in. − 6 in.
    (f) 6 ft 8 in. − 4 ft 10 in.

19. Arrange the following lengths in order.
    Start with the longest.

    | String A | 3 ft 1 in. |
    | String B | 29 in. |
    | String C | 2 ft 9 in. |
    | String D | 38 in. |

20. Jacob is 1 m 60 cm tall.
    Ryan is 16 cm shorter than Jacob.
    What is Ryan's height?

21.

Park   580 m   Library   ?   Tom's house

Tom's house is 1 km from the park.
How far is Tom's house from the library?

171

22. Mr. Cole tied two packages with these strings.

1 m 80 cm   **1 m 65 cm**

What was the total length of the strings?

23. Find the distance between the boat and the lighthouse.

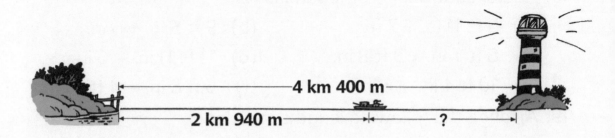

24. Mr. Marconi is 6 ft 2 in. tall.

His son Josh is 3 ft 10 in. tall.

How much shorter is Josh than his dad?

25. (a) Shane's sister wanted to know how far 7 km 2 m is in meters.

Shane told her that it is 7,002 m.

Is Shane correct? Explain your answer.

(b) Shane's mother wanted to know how long 5 feet is in inches.

Shane told her that 5 feet is 500 inches.

Is Shane correct? Explain your answer.

Review 5, pages 194–197

GLOSSARY

Word	Meaning
centimeter	The **centimeter** is a metric unit of length used for measuring short lengths. We write **cm** for centimeter. $$100 \text{ cm} = 1 \text{ m}$$
difference	To find the **difference** between two numbers, we subtract the smaller number from the greater number. $$142 - 21 = 121$$ The **difference** between 142 and 21 is 121.
estimation	When we **estimate** an answer, we round the parts of the question so that we can find an answer quickly. This gives us an answer that is about the same as the actual answer. $312 + 48$ is about $300 + 50$. Thus, the value of $312 + 48$ is about $$300 + 50 = 350$$

Word	Meaning
even numbers	Numbers in which the ones digit is 0, 2, 4, 6, or 8 are called **even numbers**.
expanded form	We write the **expanded form** of the number 4,198 like this: $$4{,}000 + 100 + 90 + 8$$
kilometer	The **kilometer** is a metric unit of length used to measure long distances. We write **km** for kilometer. $$1\,km = 1{,}000\,m$$
meter	The **meter** is a metric unit of length. We write **m** for meter. $$100\,cm = 1\,m$$ $$1{,}000\,m = 1\,km$$
mile	A **mile** is a unit of length used to measure long distances. We write **mi** for mile. $$1\,mi = 5{,}280\,ft = 1{,}760\,yd$$ $$1\,mi \approx 1{,}609\,m$$

Word	Meaning
odd numbers	Numbers in which the ones digit is 1, 3, 5, 7, or 9 are called **odd numbers**.
place	 | Thousands	Hundreds	Tens	Ones
---	---	---	---
2	1	8	3	 In **2,**183, the digit **2** is in the thousands **place**.
product	To find the **product** of two numbers, we multiply the numbers. $$42 \times 6 = 252$$ The **product** of 42 and 6 is 252.
quotient	When we divide one number by another, the answer we get is called the **quotient**. $$15 \div 3 = 5$$ The **quotient** is 5.

Word	Meaning
remainder	When we divide one number by another, the number that is left over is called the **remainder**. $16 \div 3 = 5 \text{ R } 1$ The quotient is 5. The **remainder** is 1. 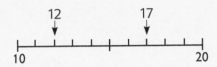 We write it as $16 \div 3 = 5 \text{ } \mathbf{R} \text{ } 1$.
rounding	When we **round** a number, we change the number to the nearest ten, nearest hundred, or nearest thousand. 12 rounded to the nearest ten is 10. 17 rounded to the nearest ten is 20.
standard form	7,639 is how we write the **standard form** of the number seven thousand, six hundred, thirty-nine.

Word	Meaning
sum	To find the **sum** of two numbers, we add the numbers together. $$142 + 21 = 163$$ The **sum** of 142 and 21 is 163.
value	The **value** of a digit in a number is the amount the digit represents in the number. In 2,**7**14, the **value** of the digit **7** is 700. The value of a missing number in an equation is the number that will make that equation true. $45 + n = 46$. The value of n is 1. The value of an expression is the answer. Find the value of 4×3. The value of 4×3 is 12.

Grade 3 Curriculum Map

Common Core State Standards		Unit	Student Textbook Pages	Student Workbook Exercises
OPERATIONS AND ALGEBRAIC THINKING				
Represent and solve problems involving multiplication and division.				
3.OA.1	Interpret products of whole numbers, e.g., interpret 5 × 7 as the total number of objects in 5 groups of 7 objects each or 7 groups of 5 objects each. *For example, describe a context in which a total number of objects can be expressed as 5 × 7.*	**Unit 3 Lesson 1 Looking Back** **Unit 4 Lesson 1 Multiplying and Dividing by 6** **Unit 4 Lesson 2 Multiplying and Dividing by 7** **Unit 4 Lesson 3 Multiplying and Dividing by 8** **Unit 4 Lesson 4 Multiplying and Dividing by 9**	**3A:** 79–83, 125–128, 132–135, 138–139, 141–143	**3A:** 75–77, 78–81, 125–126, 127–128, 139–141, 150–151, 152–153, 154–155, 160–161, 162–163, 164–165

Common Core State Standards		Unit	Student Textbook Pages	Student Workbook Exercises
3.OA.2	Interpret whole-number quotients of whole numbers, e.g., interpret 56 ÷ 8 as the number of objects in each share when 56 objects are partitioned equally into 8 shares, or as a number of shares when 56 objects are partitioned into equal shares of 8 objects each. *For example, describe a context in which a number of shares or a number of groups can be expressed as 56 ÷ 8.*	**Unit 3 Lesson 1 Looking Back** **Unit 4 Lesson 1 Multiplying and Dividing by 6** **Unit 4 Lesson 2 Multiplying and Dividing by 7** **Unit 4 Lesson 3 Multiplying and Dividing by 8** **Unit 4 Lesson 4 Multiplying and Dividing by 9**	**3A:** 83–86, 128, 135–136, 139, 143	**3A:** 78–81, 82–85, 125–126, 127–128, 139–141, 142–143, 144–145, 150–151, 152–153, 154–155, 160–161, 162–163, 164–165
3.OA.3	Use multiplication and division within 100 to solve word problems in situations involving equal groups, arrays, and measurement quantities, e.g., by using drawings and equations with a symbol for the unknown number to represent the problem.	**Unit 3 Lesson 1 Looking Back** **Unit 3 Lesson 2 More Word Problems** **Unit 3 Lesson 5 Dividing Hundreds, Tens, and Ones**	**3A:** 88–89, 90–94, 116–117	**3A:** 89–90, 91–93, 114–115

Common Core State Standards		Unit	Student Textbook Pages	Student Workbook Exercises
3.OA.4	Determine the unknown whole number in a multiplication or division equation relating three whole numbers. *For example, determine the unknown number that makes the equation true in each of the equations 8 × ? = 48, 5 = □ ÷ 3, 6 × 6 = ?.*	**Unit 3 Lesson 1 Looking Back** **Unit 3 Lesson 4 Quotient and Remainder** **Unit 3 Lesson 5 Dividing Hundreds, Tens, and Ones**	**3A:** 79–82, 84–86, 105–109, 111, 113–115	**3A:** 75–77, 82–85, 108–109, 112–113
Understand properties of multiplication and the relationship between multiplication and division.				
3.OA.5	Apply properties of operations as strategies to multiply and divide. *Examples: If 6 × 4 = 24 is known, then 4 × 6 = 24 is also known. (Commutative property of multiplication.)* *3 × 5 × 2 can be found by 3 × 5 = 15, then 15 × 2 = 30, or by 5 × 2 = 10, then 3 × 10 = 30. (Associative property of multiplication.)* *Knowing that 8 × 5 = 40 and 8 × 2 = 16, one can find 8 × 7 as 8 × (5 + 2) = (8 × 5) + (8 × 2) = 40 + 16 = 56. (Distributive property.)*	**Unit 3 Lesson 1 Looking Back** **Unit 4 Lesson 1 Multiplying and Dividing by 6** **Unit 4 Lesson 2 Multiplying and Dividing by 7** **Unit 4 Lesson 3 Multiplying and Dividing by 8** **Unit 4 Lesson 4 Multiplying and Dividing by 9**	**3A:** 80, 82–83, 85, 126–127, 133–134, 138, 141, 143	**3A:** 75–77, 78–81, 160–161, 162–163, 164–165

Common Core State Standards		Unit	Student Textbook Pages	Student Workbook Exercises
3.OA.6	Understand division as an unknown-factor problem. *For example, find 32 ÷ 8 by finding the number that makes 32 when multiplied by 8.*	**Unit 3 Lesson 1 Looking Back** **Unit 4 Lesson 1 Multiplying and Dividing by 6** **Unit 4 Lesson 2 Multiplying and Dividing by 7**	**3A:** 85, 128, 135	**3A:** 125–126, 127–128, 139–141
Multiply and divide within 100.				
3.OA.7	Fluently multiply and divide within 100, using strategies such as the relationship between multiplication and division (e.g., knowing that 8 × 5 = 40, one knows 40 ÷ 5 = 8) or properties of operations. By the end of Grade 3, know from memory all products of two one-digit numbers.	**Unit 3 Lesson 1 Looking Back** **Unit 3 Lesson 3 Multiplying Ones, Tens, and Hundreds** **Unit 3 Lesson 4 Quotient and Remainder** **Unit 3 Lesson 5 Dividing Hundreds, Tens, and Ones** **Unit 4 Lesson 1 Multiplying and Dividing by 6** **Unit 4 Lesson 2 Multiplying and Dividing by 7** **Unit 4 Lesson 3 Multiplying and Dividing by 8** **Unit 4 Lesson 4 Multiplying and Dividing by 9**	**3A:** 86–87, 89, 97, 100, 110, 114, 115, 117, 128, 130, 135–136, 139, 143	**3A:** 82–85, 86–88, 89–90, 97–98, 101–103, 110–111, 112–113, 114–115, 125–126, 127–128, 132–134, 139–141, 142–143, 144–145, 150–151, 152–153, 154–155, 160–161, 162–163, 164–165

Common Core State Standards		Unit	Student Textbook Pages	Student Workbook Exercises
Solve problems involving the four operations, and identify and explain patterns in arithmetic.				
3.OA.8	Solve two-step word problems using the four operations. Represent these problems using equations with a letter standing for the unknown quantity. Assess the reasonableness of answers using mental computation and estimation strategies including rounding.	**Unit 2 Lesson 7 Two-Step Word Problems** **Unit 3 Lesson 2 More Word Problems** **Unit 3 Lesson 5 Dividing Hundreds, Tens, and Ones** **Unit 4 Lesson 2 Multiplying and Dividing by 7** **Unit 4 Lesson 4 Multiplying and Dividing by 9** **Unit 6 Lesson 5 Word Problems**	**3A:** 66–69, 92–94, 117, 137, 144 **3B:** 27–29	**3A:** 65–67, 91–93, 114–115, 146–149, 166–169 **3B:** 24–26

Common Core State Standards		Unit	Student Textbook Pages	Student Workbook Exercises
3.OA.9	Identify arithmetic patterns (including patterns in the addition table or multiplication table), and explain them using properties of operations. *For example, observe that 4 times a number is always even, and explain why 4 times a number can be decomposed into two equal addends.*	**Unit 1 Lesson 1 Thousands, Hundreds, Tens, and Ones** **Unit 1 Lesson 2 Number Patterns** **Unit 2 Lesson 1 Mental Calculation** **Unit 3 Lesson 1 Looking Back** **Unit 4 Lesson 1 Multiplying and Dividing by 6** **Unit 4 Lesson 2 Multiplying and Dividing by 7** **Unit 4 Lesson 3 Multiplying and Dividing by 8** **Unit 4 Lesson 4 Multiplying and Dividing by 9**	**3A:** 8–11, 15–17, 29–33, 78–84, 122–123, 126–128, 133–135, 138, 139, 141–143	**3A:** 6–8, 13–15, 28–29, 30, 31–32, 75–77, 78–81, 125–126, 127–128, 139–141, 150–151, 152–153, 154–155, 160–161, 162–163, 164–165

Common Core State Standards		Unit	Student Textbook Pages	Student Workbook Exercises
NUMBER AND OPERATIONS IN BASE TEN				
Use place value understanding and properties of operations to perform multi-digit arithmetic.				
3.NBT.1	Use place value understanding to round whole numbers to the nearest 10 or 100.	**Unit 1 Lesson 3 Rounding Numbers** **Unit 2 Lesson 5 Adding Ones, Tens, Hundreds, and Thousands** **Unit 3 Lesson 3 Multiplying Ones, Tens, and Hundreds** **Unit 4 Lesson 1 Multiplying and Dividing by 6**	**3A:** 18–23, 53, 102–103, 129	**3A:** 16–17, 18–19, 53–54, 104–105, 129–131

Common Core State Standards		Unit	Student Textbook Pages	Student Workbook Exercises
3.NBT.2	Fluently add and subtract within 1,000 using strategies and algorithms based on place value, properties of operations, and/or the relationship between addition and subtraction.	**Unit 1 Lesson 1 Thousands, Hundreds, Tens, and Ones** **Unit 1 Lesson 2 Number Patterns** **Unit 2 Lesson 1 Mental Calculation** **Unit 2 Lesson 2 Looking Back: Addition and Subtraction** **Unit 2 Lesson 3 Sum and Difference** **Unit 2 Lesson 4 Word Problems** **Unit 2 Lesson 5 Adding Ones, Tens, Hundreds, and Thousands** **Unit 2 Lesson 6 Subtracting Ones, Tens, Hundreds, and Thousands** **Unit 5 Lesson 1 Meters and Centimeters** **Unit 5 Lesson 2 Kilometers** **Unit 5 Lesson 3 Other Units of Length**	**3A:** 8–12, 15–17, 29–35, 36–38, 39–44, 45–49, 50–56, 57–65, 151–152, 157–162, 164–167	**3A:** 6–8, 9–10, 13–15, 28–29, 30, 31–32, 33, 34–35, 36–37, 38–39, 40–41, 42–43, 44, 45–47, 48–50, 51–52, 53–54, 55–56, 57–58, 59–60, 61–62, 63–64, 176, 177, 181–184, 185–186, 187–189, 190, 191–192

Common Core State Standards		Unit	Student Textbook Pages	Student Workbook Exercises
3.NBT.3	Multiply one-digit whole numbers by multiples of 10 in the range 10–90 (e.g., 9 × 80, 5 × 60) using strategies based on place value and properties of operations.	**Unit 3 Lesson 3 Multiplying Ones, Tens, and Hundreds**	**3A:** 96–99, 101	**3A:** 97–98, 99–100
NUMBER AND OPERATIONS—FRACTIONS				
Develop understanding of fractions as numbers.				
3.NF.1	Understand a fraction 1/*b* as the quantity formed by 1 part when a whole is partitioned into *b* equal parts; understand a fraction *a/b* as the quantity formed by *a* parts of size 1/*b*.	**Unit 9 Lesson 1 Fraction of a Whole** **Unit 9 Lesson 4 Fraction of a Set**	**3B:** 85–86, 103–106	**3B:** 83–86, 107–108, 109–110
3.NF.2a	Understand a fraction as a number on the number line; represent fractions on a number line diagram. Represent a fraction 1/*b* on a number line diagram by defining the interval from 0 to 1 as the whole and partitioning it into *b* equal parts. Recognize that each part has size 1/*b* and that the endpoint of the part based at 0 locates the number 1/*b* on the number line.	**Unit 9 Lesson 1 Fraction of a Whole**	**3B:** 90	**3B:** 89–93
3.NF.2b	Understand a fraction as a number on the number line; represent fractions on a number line diagram. Represent a fraction *a/b* on a number line diagram by marking off *a* lengths 1/*b* from 0. Recognize that the resulting interval has size *a/b* and that its endpoint locates the number *a/b* on the number line.	**Unit 9 Lesson 1 Fraction of a Whole**	**3B:** 90	**3B:** 89–93
3.NF.3a	Explain equivalence of fractions in special cases, and compare fractions by reasoning about their size. Understand two fractions as equivalent (equal) if they are the same size, or the same point on a number line.	**Unit 9 Lesson 2 Equivalent Fractions**	**3B:** 92–94	**3B:** 94–96

Common Core State Standards		Unit	Student Textbook Pages	Student Workbook Exercises
3.NF.3b	Explain equivalence of fractions in special cases, and compare fractions by reasoning about their size. Recognize and generate simple equivalent fractions, e.g., 1/2 = 2/4, 4/6 = 2/3. Explain why the fractions are equivalent, e.g., by using a visual fraction model.	**Unit 9 Lesson 2 Equivalent Fractions**	**3B:** 95–97	**3B:** 97–98, 99–100, 101–102
3.NF.3c	Explain equivalence of fractions in special cases, and compare fractions by reasoning about their size. Express whole numbers as fractions, and recognize fractions that are equivalent to whole numbers. *Examples: Express 3 in the form 3 = 3/1; recognize that 6/1 = 6; locate 4/4 and 1 at the same point of a number line diagram.*	**Unit 9 Lesson 2 Equivalent Fractions**	**3B:** 94, 95	**3B:** 97–98
3.NF.3d	Explain equivalence of fractions in special cases, and compare fractions by reasoning about their size. Compare two fractions with the same numerator or the same denominator by reasoning about their size. Recognize that comparisons are valid only when the two fractions refer to the same whole. Record the results of comparisons with the symbols >, =, or <, and justify the conclusions, e.g., by using a visual fraction model.	**Unit 9 Lesson 2 Equivalent Fractions**	**3B:** 97–98	**3B:** 103
MEASUREMENT AND DATA				
Solve problems involving measurement and estimation of intervals of time, liquid volumes, and masses of objects.				
3.MD.1	Tell and write time to the nearest minute and measure time intervals in minutes. Solve word problems involving addition and subtraction of time intervals in minutes, e.g., by representing the problem on a number line diagram.	**Unit 10 Lesson 1 Hours and Minutes**	**3B:** 113–121	**3B:** 115–116, 117–118, 119–120, 121–122, 123–124, 125–126

Common Core State Standards		Unit	Student Textbook Pages	Student Workbook Exercises
3.MD.2	Measure and estimate liquid volumes and masses of objects using standard units of grams (g), kilograms (kg), and liters (l). Add, subtract, multiply, or divide to solve one-step word problems involving masses or volumes that are given in the same units, e.g., by using drawings (such as a beaker with a measurement scale) to represent the problem.	**Unit 6 Lesson 2 Measuring Mass in Kilograms** **Unit 6 Lesson 3 Measuring Mass in Grams** **Unit 6 Lesson 4 Kilograms and Grams** **Unit 6 Lesson 5 Word Problems** **Unit 7 Lesson 1 Comparing Capacity** **Unit 7 Lesson 2 Liters** **Unit 7 Lesson 3 Liters and Milliliters** **Unit 7 Lesson 4 Gallons, Quarts, Pints, and Cups**	**3B:** 10–14, 15–18, 20–24, 26–29, 42–62	**3B:** 9–12, 17, 18–20, 21–23, 24–26, 37–39, 40, 41–44, 45–46, 47–48, 49–53, 54–55, 56–57, 58

Common Core State Standards		Unit	Student Textbook Pages	Student Workbook Exercises
Represent and interpret data.				
3.MD.3	Draw a scaled picture graph and a scaled bar graph to represent a data set with several categories. Solve one- and two-step "how many more" and "how many less" problems using information presented in scaled bar graphs. *For example, draw a bar graph in which each square in the bar graph might represent 5 pets.*	**Unit 11 Lesson 1 Presenting Data**	**3B:** 129–132	**3B:** 138–144
3.MD.4	Generate measurement data by measuring lengths using rulers marked with halves and fourths of an inch. Show the data by making a line plot, where the horizontal scale is marked off in appropriate units—whole numbers, halves, or quarters.	**Unit 11 Lesson 1 Presenting Data**	**3B:** 133	**3B:** 145–146
Geometric measurement: understand concepts of area and relate area to multiplication and to addition.				
3.MD.5a	Recognize area as an attribute of plane figures and understand concepts of area measurement. A square with side length 1 unit, called "a unit square," is said to have "one square unit" of area, and can be used to measure area.	**Unit 13 Lesson 1 Area**	**3B:** 144–147	**3B:** 158–161, 162–166
3.MD.5b	Recognize area as an attribute of plane figures and understand concepts of area measurement. A plane figure which can be covered without gaps or overlaps by *n* unit squares is said to have an area of *n* square units.	**Unit 13 Lesson 1 Area** **Unit 13 Lesson 3 Area of a Rectangle** **Unit 13 Lesson 4 Composite Figures**	**3B:** 144–151, 157–160, 161–164	**3B:** 158–161, 162–166, 167–170, 175–177, 178–180

Common Core State Standards		Unit	Student Textbook Pages	Student Workbook Exercises
3.MD.6	Measure areas by counting unit squares (square cm, square m, square in, square ft, and improvised units).	**Unit 13 Lesson 1 Area**	**3B:** 144 –150	**3B:** 158–161, 162–166, 167–170
3.MD.7a	Relate area to the operations of multiplication and addition. Find the area of a rectangle with whole-number side lengths by tiling it, and show that the area is the same as would be found by multiplying the side lengths.	**Unit 13 Lesson 3 Area of a Rectangle**	**3B:** 157–158	
3.MD.7b	Relate area to the operations of multiplication and addition. Multiply side lengths to find areas of rectangles with whole-number side lengths in the context of solving real world and mathematical problems, and represent whole-number products as rectangular areas in mathematical reasoning.	**Unit 13 Lesson 3 Area of a Rectangle**	**3B:** 159–160	**3B:** 175–177
3.MD.7c	Relate area to the operations of multiplication and addition. Use tiling to show in a concrete case that the area of a rectangle with whole-number side lengths a and $b + c$ is the sum of $a \times b$ and $a \times c$. Use area models to represent the distributive property in mathematical reasoning.	**Unit 13 Lesson 4 Composite Figures**	**3B:** 163	
3.MD.7d	Relate area to the operations of multiplication and addition. Recognize area as additive. Find areas of rectilinear figures by decomposing them into non-overlapping rectangles and adding the areas of the non-overlapping parts, applying this technique to solve real world problems.	**Unit 13 Lesson 4 Composite Figures**	**3B:** 164	**3B:** 178–180

Common Core State Standards		Unit	Student Textbook Pages	Student Workbook Exercises
Geometric measurement: recognize perimeter as an attribute of plane figures and distinguish between linear and area measures.				
3.MD.8	Solve real world and mathematical problems involving perimeters of polygons, including finding the perimeter given the side lengths, finding an unknown side length, and exhibiting rectangles with the same perimeter and different areas or with the same area and different perimeters.	**Unit 13 Lesson 2 Perimeter** **Unit 13 Lesson 4 Composite Figures**	**3B:** 153–156, 161	**3B:** 171–172, 173–174
GEOMETRY				
Reason with shapes and their attributes.				
3.G.1	Understand that shapes in different categories (e.g., rhombuses, rectangles, and others) may share attributes (e.g., having four sides), and that the shared attributes can define a larger category (e.g., quadrilaterals). Recognize rhombuses, rectangles, and squares as examples of quadrilaterals, and draw examples of quadrilaterals that do not belong to any of these subcategories.	**Unit 12 Lesson 1 Right Angles and Shapes**	**3B:** 140	**3B:** 153–155
3.G.2	Partition shapes into parts with equal areas. Express the area of each part as a unit fraction of the whole. *For example, partition a shape into 4 parts with equal area, and describe the area of each part as 1/4 of the area of the shape.*	**Unit 9 Lesson 1 Fraction of a Whole**	**3B:** 86–89	**3B:** 83–88

Index